DATE DUE

DEMCO 38-296

MODERN TUNISIA

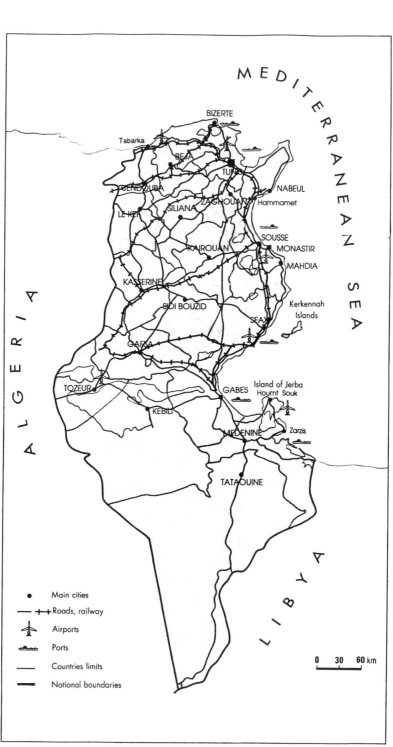

Map of Tunisia

MODERN TUNISIA

A Democratic Apprenticeship

Andrew Borowiec

Westport, Connecticut
London

Library of Congress Cataloging-in-Publication Data

Borowiec, Andrew.
    Modern Tunisia : a democratic apprenticeship / Andrew Borowiec.
      p. cm.
    Includes bibliographical references (p.) and index.
    ISBN 0–275–96136–2 (alk. paper)
    1. Tunisia—Politics and government. I. Title.
DT264.46.B67   1998
320.9611—dc21   97–32948

British Library Cataloguing in Publication Data is available.

Library of Congress Catalog Card Number: 97–32948
ISBN: 0–275–96136–2

First published in 1998

Praeger Publishers, 88 Post Road West, Westport, CT 06881
An imprint of Greenwood Publishing Group, Inc.

Printed in the United States of America

The paper used in this book complies with the
Permanent Paper Standard issued by the National
Information Standards Organization (Z39.48–1984).

10 9 8 7 6 5 4 3 2 1

For Juliet, again

Contents

Preface

While parts of this book are based on my personal experience and notes preserved during years of reporting in the area, the latest data and pertaining statements could not have been obtained without the help of the Tunisian authorities. The Tunisian External Communications Agency opened its archives to my scrutiny and was instrumental in arranging numerous interviews with key officials, including ten members of the cabinet.

My special thanks go to Noureddine Dougui, head of the Institut Supérieur d'Histoire du Mouvement National, for his analysis of Tunisia's 19th- and 20th-century history; to Abdelbaki Hermassi, the minister of culture, whose comments and work "The Islamic Dilemma" were particularly pertaining; and to Nejib Benlazreg, an archaeologist whose portrayal of Tunisia's early past was exceptionally fascinating.

Once again, I thank my wife Juliet for her careful editing and Chris Haber who led me through the minefield of cybernetics to make the manuscript presentable.

A word about the spelling of Arabic names and terms used in the text. Transliteration from the Arabic alphabet is a daunting task, and experts often resort to the transmutation of sounds to better reflect the original. This has led to frequent changes in which newspapers and other publications have indulged with gusto. For example, the name of Libya's strongman has been transformed from Qadhafi to Kaddafi and finally to Gadhafi, although other imaginative ways of spelling it are also being used. Egypt's President Mubarak can be Hosni or Husni. The most popular Arabic name has been spelled Mohammed, Mohamed, Muhamad, or even M'hammed (the last favored by Algeria's former information minister, M'hammed Yazid).

I have opted for the easiest formula, that used by Tunisia's French-language press and official documents which translate the Arabic into the Latin alphabet the way the French have done it. Thus it is Hocine and not Hosseyn and Noureddine and not Nur'din. The market is a souk and not a suq, the latter preferred by many Western Arabists. The city known for its mosque, carpets, and Aghlabite forts is Kairouan and not Qarwuan, and Bourguiba is Bourguiba, despite the fact that in some books he has been Bourguibah or even Bur-qiba. I have made an exception in the case of the port city north of Tunis which is Bizerte to Tunisians but Bizerta on most English-language maps and World War II documents. The rather notorious Islamic leader is Ghannouchi (as well as his namesake who is a cabinet member in Tunisia) and not Ghannoushi, as in some English-language texts.

Introduction

This book is about present-day Tunisia, an Arab, Muslim, and North African country with strong European links and aspirations. It is a country steeped in tradition honed by three millennia and polished by French culture during the colonial period. Somewhat incongruously, its penchant for Western civilization and values increased after independence, perhaps because such values were no longer imposed by the colonial power. Today children in distant villages begin to learn French at the age of eight, and Tunisian intellectuals are equally at ease in Paris as they are in Tunis or Sfax. Increasingly, Tunisians are learning English, a language associated with success in business and sciences.

While volumes have been written about Tunisia's ancient history, relatively little is known in the United States about its contemporary struggle and the many challenges it has had to confront. The international press is generally preoccupied with drama. On the whole, Tunisia has been spared dramatic upheaval and even its handling of major political changes and the struggle against Islamic fundamentalism has been relatively low key. I thought that perhaps the time was ripe to paint an up-to-date picture of modern Tunisia as it approaches the new century.

As an Associated Press correspondent in North Africa, I had the opportunity to witness Tunisia's first, hesitant steps as an independent nation and its subsequent trials and tribulations. Four of those years were spent in Tunis, and my relationship with the government was not always a happy one. The Tunisian authorities in those days had a different concept of the press, and some felt that my news dispatches were not "helping the cause of Tunisian-

American friendship." On two occasions, as Tunisia experimented with socialism, it was suggested that I leave the country. The suggestion was never translated into action and I eventually left in the normal course of events for another assignment, to return, however, to Tunisia on many occasions during the subsequent 30 years, without hindrance.

In this study, I decided to concentrate almost exclusively on the post-independence period and particularly on the last ten years after the removal from power of Habib Bourguiba, a senile president-for-life to whom, nonetheless, Tunisia owes a great deal. It was Bourguiba who launched the country on the path of social and educational reforms that were to bring it closer to the Western world. Unfortunately, Tunisia's "Supreme Warrior" overstayed his time and the country's welcome and became a victim of old age and of power-hungry courtiers. In 1987, the then prime minister, Zine El Abidine Ben Ali, constitutionally removed Bourguiba from his position, invoking his senility and inability to govern. Bourguiba's reforms were, nonetheless, preserved and expanded, and he was treated with respect. The way the transfer of power was handled showed considerable maturity, which impressed a number of world capitals. In Tunisia's current political vocabulary, the event has become known as the Change.

Thus this book is mainly about the Change. It intends to show how it affected the life of the country and of its nine million people. It analyzes Tunisia's concept of "presidential democracy" and outlines plans for its evolution into a multi-party system. It points out that the period of "democratic apprenticeship" is far from over and that external threat, mainly from Islamic fundamentalist extremists, continues to weigh over Tunisia. It shows that, devoid of natural wealth although blessed with a mild climate, proximity to Europe and an educated population, Tunisia is perhaps the only Arab country without oil that is capable of reaching the stage of becoming a "young developed nation" in the not too distant future.

Above all, this book is about Tunisians: erudite scholars, eminent Arabists, French-speaking technocrats, merchants of Bab Sadoun, fishmongers of La Goulette, and Jewish silversmiths of Djerba. It is about burnoused shepherds in the hills of central Tunisia, their faces burnished the color of copper by the merciless sun and wind. It is about women fighting for control of privatized enterprises, students waiting at bus stops on gray autumnal mornings and crowds applauding singers during jasmine-scented summer evenings in the seaside cafes of La Marsa, and about their president and his plans for the future, his cabinet members, and the swelling ranks of the Tunisian middle class.

Throughout Ben Ali's mandate and a system known as "presidential democracy," questions have been raised in Western chanceries about the extent of democratic procedure in Tunisia and the extent to which the country's citizens are able to influence the power structure. Critics, including the U.S. State Department, claim "the ability of the citizens to change the government is yet to be demonstrated."[1] The regime retorts that the opposition, particularly the Islamic one, is mainly destructive and has no valid alternative to the government's progressive social and economic policies. Thus the only opposition authorized is the one that subscribes to Ben Ali's program. As this work was being written, there was little doubt that all significant decisions in Tunisia emanated from the presidential palace in Carthage. The Tunisian president was not answerable to the press which, in effect, was hardly more than the regime's organ. Protected by a highly conspicuous wall of security, he was not easily accessible to either Tunisian citizens or foreigners. This work attempts to explain how the government justifies such measures in the atmosphere of "siege" by the country's unstable and controversial neighbors, Algeria and Libya, and the threat of Islamic extremists. In the two elections held since Bourguiba's removal, Ben Ali was the only presidential candidate, an act officially explained as guaranteeing political stability and security, both essential to Tunisia's progress. Again, this book will attempt to shed more light on this concept, basically contrary to the Western view of democratic procedure.

NOTE

1. U.S. State Department report, January 1997.

CHAPTER 1

Change of Guard

It was that hour between Al-Fajr and Ach-Chourouq, the first two prayers of the day, when flower vendors open their stalls on the Avenue Habib Bourguiba in the center of Tunis and fishing boats head back to Cap Bon. The time was 6:30 A.M., and the date November 7, 1987.

A chronicler of that period described the day as "banal, chilly and greyish." In some ways it was an ordinary autumnal morning in Tunisia, but unusual in others: it was the day that ended one era and ushered in a new one.

Tunis radio began its programs with ballads and folk music. Those who listened recall the absence of rousing marches or of the usual paeans to Habib Bourguiba, the founder of modern Tunisia and its "president-for-life." Now a man whose attention span at the age of 84 lasted barely two hours a day during which period he signed decrees or canceled them, according to the moods of the courtiers surrounding him in his Carthage palace.

The first to speak on the air was an announcer. In an emotion-charged voice, he introduced the prime minister of the previous few weeks, Zine El Abidine Ben Ali.

No, it was not the news of Bourguiba's death, as many listeners had thought. The prime minister announced "in the name of God, the Compassionate, the Merciful," that because of the increasing senility of the president, "national duty" forced him to declare Bourguiba to be "totally incapable of carrying out the duties of the president of the republic." In doing so, Ben Ali said, on the basis of Article 57 of the constitution, "with

God's help we are taking charge of the presidency of the republic and supreme command of our armed forces."

The news was not a surprise and, as one senior official said later, "it was either Bourguiba or Ben Ali." While foreign chanceries took some time to approve of what several envoys initially spoke of as a "palace coup," later all agreed that Ben Ali saved the North African country of nine million, nestled between Algeria and Libya, from a possible disaster.

Many expected bloodshed, turmoil, and fratricidal struggle for Bourguiba's shaky heritage. Nothing of the sort happened because what took place on that gray November morning was not a *putsch* but an operation to save the country from an uncertain fate.

The state coffers were literally empty, and Tunisia had no money to service its foreign debt. Successive prime ministers had had their hands tied by what a senior official described later as a "government by (Bourguiba's) seraglio." The man who had charmed world capitals with his famous blue gaze and bold secular reforms resembling those of Turkey's Mustafa Kemal Ataturk, had become a *pantin*—a puppet.

Nine years later, Mustapha Khammari, director of the Dar Assabah publishing company in Tunis, recalled the general mood of the country which for years had felt adrift and rudderless. "There was total political instability, the national conscience was in danger. We knew that such a situation had to end and it could have ended violently. But we managed to stop just at the edge of a precipice."[1]

At that time the imminent danger to Bourguiba and, indeed to his successor, was the growing Islamic fundamentalist movement which had succeeded in infiltrating schools, mosques, universities, and the armed forces, the latter to a lesser but potentially more dangerous extent. Indeed, the well-entrenched Islamic apparatus was poised to seize power just the day after Ben Ali removed the old "Combattant Suprême" from his palace. Bourguiba believed in only one way of dealing with the militant Islamists: send them to the gallows or lock them up for life. Ben Ali's pleas, as a newly installed prime minister, to exercise mercy and to try to co-opt some opponents, had little effect on the aging leader.

Many Tunisians felt that Bourguiba's inability to govern was one of the main reasons for the growth of the Islamic movement. Abdelbaki Hermassi, a university professor who served as Minister of Culture in the post-Bourguiba cabinets, observed that "the economic frustration during the period of autocratic and senile regime" was one of the key factors in the rise of Tunisian fundamentalism, eventually stifled by a combination of reforms and tough security measures during the first years of Ben Ali's presidency.[2]

But at the time of Bourguiba's "gentle but unceremonious" removal, the Islamic problem was far from settled. It took about five years of political maneuvering and stern measures before the Tunisian officials announced that the country had been "vaccinated" against fundamentalism.

The beginning of what has become known in the official Tunisian vocabulary as "the Change" was marked by a series of salutary economic measures that eventually restored the confidence of the country's potential economic partners as well as of the international lending organizations. While a debate as to the degree of democracy in the Tunisian "presidential system" continues in foreign capitals, no one denies the success of the country's economic effort despite the initially destructive fundamentalist threat.

Ben Ali's task was facilitated by a consensus among Tunisia's educated elite and officialdom who firmly believed—and still do—that the Islamists clamoring for a political voice want democracy only in order to establish a medieval theocracy. The regimes in Tehran, Kabul, and Khartoum are cited as vivid examples.

According to Sadok Chaabane, a law professor who became minister of justice in 1996, the fundamentalist movements want "neither mending nor reforming" but simply plan to "change society from top to bottom, seize power and use the state apparatus for their own aims."[3]

Chaabane believes that for some years before Ben Ali's move, basically since the end of the 1960s, Tunisian society "continued to accumulate rancor and anger" while impotence reached the top levers of the state, having first "paralyzed the entire regime."

Compounding the weakness of the Bourguiba government in its waning years was the emergence of militant Islam. It was a period during which the West started conceiving Islam as being on a "collision course" with any form of secular governance in predominantly Muslim countries. In the West itself, Islamic fundamentalism started being regarded as "a triple threat: political, demographic and socioreligious."[4]

Tunisia's fragility in those years was further increased by the unstable nature of its neighbors, Libya and Algeria, amidst an intense feeling in the educated spheres that those two countries were in a position to harm—indeed, destroy—the Tunisian achievements by their very proximity and unclear objectives. Such concern was unquestionably increased, even after Ben Ali's takeover, as Algeria began to grapple with Islamic forces, radicalized in the mid-1990s.

Thus on the eve of Ben Ali's dramatic move in November 1987, a strong national consensus felt that there was no such thing as moderate fundamentalism; the Islamists had a totalitarian view of politics, including a "seizure of power with authority over life, death and morality."[5]

The prospect of an inevitable clash between a politically paralyzed Bourguiba and his prime minister was shaping up in an idyllic Mediterranean setting. Tunisia was firmly on the world tourism map, with its incomparable Punic and Roman ruins, its mild climate, its miles of sandy beaches, and its Western-oriented population. An ambitious expansion of tourism, started in the late 1950s, attracted a growing number of foreign visitors annually (the figure reached four million nine years after Ben Ali's take-over). The hotel infrastructure kept up with the high demand.

Bourguiba himself was a respected international figure, virtually unique in the Arab world. He was enlightened, erudite, often charming, easily accessible to foreign visitors and hardly security conscious. The personality cult he had created around himself was seen in the West as an inseparable part of the "Arab way" of governing. Western capitals were generally oblivious to the intrigues around the "Supreme Warrior" simmering daily in his Carthage palace as well as in the other elaborate presidential residences. Occasional reports of scheming and manipulation by courtiers were described by Tunisian diplomats as mere *cafe klatsch,* although the question of the president's succession was a gnawing subject to most Tunisians.

The problem was of considerable magnitude by the simple fact that for 31 years Tunisia had lived under Bourguiba's unquestionably autocratic rule. The achievements of the "father of the nation" were considerable after he led the country to independence from French rule in 1956. Officially known as a protectorate, in effect Tunisia was ruled as a French colony. "An indefatigable reformer" according to most observers of the initial period after independence, Bourguiba launched the country on the path of progress, stressing compulsory education, emancipation of women, and generally succeeding in turning the country "from a backward, impoverished state into a model of social progress."[6] This was accomplished even though Tunisia suffered fallout of the war of independence in neighboring Algeria and launched a costly experiment with socialism, followed by unfettered liberalism which further strained its resources and economic progress.

During his last years in power, Bourguiba showed definite signs of senility, cleverly exploited by wily courtiers who succeeded in exerting considerable influence on the man whom many Tunisians for years considered to be a "grand monsieur." Eventually the situation, while unquestionably dramatic, bordered on the grotesque. "Almost every morning we awaited news that yet another man appointed the day before would be relieved of his duties in a continuing struggle for palace influence," recalled one Tunisian. During those last years Bourguiba frequently forgot the names of his cabinet members and grew increasingly erratic. These were not factors to help the country's morale or stability.

The most Westernized country in the Arab world and by far the most progressive, deprived of leadership at a crucial period when militant Islam had begun spreading its tentacles throughout the area, Tunisia staggered through uncertainty. Many Tunisians were clearly embarrassed by the atmosphere on top of the ruling pyramid. No one dared speculate in public about the president's successor. The act of governing was, at best, an ad hoc operation. During the months preceding his removal from power, Bourguiba appointed and fired three prime ministers in quick succession. And, apparently, he was ready to dismiss Ben Ali whom he accused of being too lenient with Islamic fundamentalists. And yet it was Ben Ali who, as interior minister before his appointment to the premiership, seriously crippled the Islamist movement by decapitating its leadership and destroying a number of cells of the Islamic Tendency Movement (*Mouvement de la Tendance Islamique*—French initials MTI).

It was clear that solutions were needed, some of them desperately. The struggle to limit militant Islam, effective to some extent until Bourguiba's departure, was not sufficient, without profound reforms, to deprive the opposition, mainly Islamic, from its source of power—an increasingly dissatisfied population.

The answer came some months after the advent of the "Change," in the form of economic and political measures applied by Ben Ali with considerable profusion. They included the replacement of the official Socialist Destour Party with the Constitutional Democratic ally (*Rassemblement Constitutionnel Démocratique*—RCD), the "National Pact" under which the recognized political forces formally subscribed to Ben Ali's program, and measures to liberalize the economic structure combined with encouragement of foreign investments. The program continued during the entire first decade of the Change, with general applause from Western capitals, encouragement from investors, and envy by what has become known as other "new democracies."

Much more was to be built on the damaged edifice of the Tunisian state. But according to Habib Ben Yahia, long-time Tunisian ambassador to Japan, Great Britain, and the United States and subsequent minister of foreign affairs and defense, "we had a national consensus, social peace and no desire to flirt with a violent terrorist movement. Besides, religion should not be propagated with a machinegun. Democracy should not be based on citations from the Koran."[7]

Other factors of the Change included a halt to the demographic time-bomb, which was started by Bourguiba but had become lax in later years, and a stress on Tunisia's "Mediterranean vocation," one of Ben Ali's favorite themes, which he repeats at international conferences and meetings with business leaders. Tunisia, clearly, has shelved prospects of closer cooperation with African and Arab nations, basing its future course on strictly pragmatic considerations.

As the government seriously limited the field of action of the Islamic forces, driving them underground or into exile, there were some doubts in Western chanceries whether the threat from the fundamentalists was as serious as the government believed. Skeptics claimed that the danger was "exaggerated" to facilitate restrictive measures and give the government a free hand in dealing with economic and other internal problems. Most Tunisians interviewed at the time of Ben Ali's takeover and during the subsequent years, firmly reject such a theory. The rise of militant and institutionalized Islam was seen by them as the worst threat to the republic and its system, its inevitable imperfections notwithstanding. Years later, Tunisians—and that includes high-ranking government officials—still spoke of the country's "democratic apprenticeship." The most common view among men and women backing the Ben Ali regime was that "the Tunisian democracy is still young and the struggle continues. Each country has its own sense of timing and priorities. We need time—and the benefit of doubt."[8]

Nonetheless, during the first three years of the Change, three new secular opposition parties received official authorization to function and put up candidates in elections. Subsequently, this "legal opposition" was given limited representation in the Chamber of Deputies, the country's parliament, based on the modification of the electoral system (see Chapter 6). Such parties subscribed to the National Pact between the political forces and the government and did not get out of step. There were indications that their field of action would increase with time. Obviously, and at least for the time being, "the benefit of doubt" was needed.

The official view during the first period of the Change was that giving a free rein to all political forces would be tantamount to national suicide, or at least to the destruction of the Tunisian system. Tunisian officials like to recall the chaos that replaced communism in some East European countries as well as the more glaring example of nearby Algeria, a country whose torment during the 1990s remained a major cloud over Tunisia's own future. Algeria "opened the road to pluralism without foreseeing its immediate political fallout. Thus, more than 60 political parties were created within one month."[9] At the time of Algeria's decision, Abdallah Kallel, Tunisian minister of Justice, warned Chedli Ben Jedid, Algeria's president, of the danger looming before his country. Ben Jedid "replied coldly" that each country was free to chose its options."[10] The Algerian head of state was forced to resign a few months after that meeting, on January 11, 1992. Algeria was plunged into a seemingly endless series of terrorist attacks for years to come.

Ben Ali, obviously, chose his own "option," which spared Tunisia a similar fate. When Tunisian Islamists scored gains in the 1989 elections, Ben Ali was under some external pressure to "recognize their strength."[11] The Tunisian president rejected all such efforts at diplomatic persuasion, pointing out that no lasting compromise with extremist forces was possible—or even imaginable.

While several years later Ben Ali's views were to a great extent vindicated, Algeria's problems and its reactions to radical Islam caused further "soul-searching" among Western policy makers, politicians, and members of what has become known as "think tanks." In a way, the situation seemed incongruous. When, in December 1991, Algeria's Islamic Salvation Front (*Front Islamique de Salut*—FIS) won the first round of legislative elections and was poised to win the second round set for January, Western capitals feared the worst. After all, Algeria was not distant Iran with its mullahs barricaded behind Koranic verses or Sudan engulfed in a series of civil wars for more than three decades. Algeria used to be "an extension of France" (according to French slogans from the colonial era), had established good relations with European countries after independence and, above all, was an hour's flight from Marseille by commercial jet. The idea of an Islamic regime in Algiers, especially given the large Algerian community in France, suddenly loomed as a security nightmare.

Hence, the removal of Ben Jedid as president and the decision by his military successors on January 11, 1992, to cancel the second round of the vote, was greeted in Western capitals with a sigh of relief. The specter of a hostile Islamic power at Europe's southern gates was removed, although politicians of various persuasions carefully refrained from giving open support to Algeria's new rulers. Such a cautious approach to Algeria's travail remained for years, during which time in Tunisia U.S. diplomats tried to persuade President Ben Ali that "democracy should take its course." Furthermore, American diplomats argued with their Tunisian and Algerian counterparts, if the Islamists are really that strong, they should be allowed to try their hand at governing and, once they have shown their ineptness, they will be defeated at the polls.

Such reasoning, while unquestionably valid on the banks of the Potomac, was anathema to Algerian and Tunisian leaders alike, faced as they were with what was tantamount to an armed and brutal insurrection (although in Tunisia it was stifled virtually at the beginning). In the end, both the Algerians and Tunisians ignored the preaching of their American friends, no matter how well intentioned and "politically correct." But, while Algeria resorted mainly to repression and military action, Tunisia opted for a multi-pronged strategy of reform, education, and only restrained punishment for Islamist opponents who, from the legal point of view, violated the country's strict code banning religion as a political weapon or platform.

During the crucial years of the 1990s, Western democracies felt a "visible sense of relief coupled with an embarrassed sense that it was clearly hypocritical to applaud the reversal by force of a democratic mandate."[12] In a nutshell, the issue was what happens "when a nondemocratic government comes to power by democratic means?" During the next eight years no one managed to come up with a satisfactory answer—and no one was likely to.

In the face of Algeria's slaughter, which continued well into the decade in striking contrast with Tunisia's tranquil march toward a developed and democratic society, Western thinkers still debated whether an Islamic movement was necessarily anti-democratic. Again, and countless times, Tunisian officials pointed to the constrictions of the religious regimes in Muslim countries. Under Ben Ali's rule, the watchword became "a genuine Islam against a fanatical Islam." Such a perception, approved by the entire legal political spectrum, accompanied Ben Ali's reforms. According to Hedi Mechri, director of the economic journal *L'Economiste Maghrebin*, "because of the Islamist movement, religion in Arab countries has assumed a greater role than before. Consequently, government gestures toward religion are essential. In short, governments need to pull the rug from under the fundamentalists."[13]

Ben Ali's approach to this problem had some critics in the West who tended to judge Tunisia's "democratic apprenticeship" from a distant, Western perspective, often ignoring the realities on the ground. The key issue here was the overwhelming role of the "presidential system" under which the head of state made most if not all crucial decisions, and the absence of a critical parliament that could challenge the Carthage palace. Such a concept would be hard to conceive in the conditions of Tunisia, a country which, for practical purposes, was in a state of siege—from Islamic forces in Algeria eager to export their revolution and from the erratic behavior of Colonel Gadhafi in Libya. Besides, Tunisian officials kept reminding their friends that their democracy was still fragile and in a state of constant evolution.

The overriding idea in Ben Ali's policies toward religion and, obviously in Tunisia's case, toward Islam, was that "mosques belong to God and God only, and that no political movement should have the exclusive right to use religion for its aims." During his early period in power, Bourguiba's successor firmly believed that the fundamentalist movement played on traditional Arab nationalism and exploited its weaknesses and passions. This, according to official explanations, was the reason for Ben Ali's resistance to a multi-party system that would include Islamic fundamentalists.

While some critics of Ben Ali's policies remained vocal throughout the first ten years of the Change, mainly from abroad, no major opposition emerged inside Tunisia. Tunisian officials often claimed that foreign-based "professional dissidents" were totally irrelevant at home and that they were given undue attention abroad. In any case, most Tunisians simply have not been used to any form of political criticism since the country's independence from French rule in 1956. There was also a theory (propagated by officials) that Ben Ali's policies were so beneficial to Tunisia that there was no ground for criticism.

Despite government subsidies, the handful of opposition newspapers was unable to attract sizeable readership. Their limited impact was further diminished by sweeping sociopolitical changes that followed Bourguiba's departure from the political scene.

Comments from abroad varied and, for example, included an article in *Le Monde Diplomatique*, an organ of the respected French liberal daily *Le Monde*, which, while praising the Ben Ali regime's economic achievements, attributed their success to the repression of the Islamic movement as well as to the country's saturation with a police force which had risen "in several months from 20,000 to 80,000 personnel."[14] Such a figure, for a population of a little over nine million, seemed hard to believe and was discarded by the authorities as hostile propaganda. (*Le Monde*, which refused to print various official Tunisian letters protesting against its coverage, has on occasion been banned in Tunisia.)

In his *Renaissance or Radicalism?*, a study of political Islam in Tunisia, Michael Dunn states that Ben Ali "though a military security man by training, has in many respects had a better record than did Bourguiba on human rights issues: he has encouraged openness and appointed advisors on the subject."[15]

In any analysis of modern Tunisia, particular attention should be paid to its "francophonie" (French speaking), a factor with a deep impact on the country's policies and intellectual orientation. This, in some respects, has led to a form of split personality: the Tunisians are Arabs and the educated ones seem to be more at ease in France than in Arab countries. They speak Arabic at home (most often its Tunisian version), but on certain subjects they prefer to express themselves in French. In general, French cannot be considered a foreign language in Tunisia where even in isolated villages children begin to learn it at the age of eight. Recently, the teaching of English was introduced on a large scale, but its impact is yet to be felt. In any case, knowledge of the French language is, perhaps, the most tangible heritage of the French colonial era. It has linked Tunisia with Europe, and brought its educated elite closer to those of European countries. It has become Tunisia's "window on the world," something Ben Ali has preserved despite some inevitable tiffs with the former colonial power which diminished as the memories of colonial domination were relegated to history books.

History is becoming an increasingly respected subject in Tunisian education. It no longer concentrates on Arab conquests and Turkish caliphs but includes the entire period that has marked Tunisia, from the Phoenicians through Greeks, Romans, and others who made an impression on Tunisian soil. In fact, it is impossible to assess or analyze the events of modern-age Tunisia without a glance at the periods that have influenced its people and their culture.

NOTES

1. Mustapha Khammari in conversation with the author.
2. Ibid.
3. Sadok Chaabane, *Ben Ali et la Voie Pluraliste en Tunisie* (Tunis: Ceres Editions, 1996), p. 36.
4. John L. Esposito, *The Islamic Threat: Myth or Reality?* (New York: Oxford University Press, 1992), p. 175.
5. Abdelbaki Hermassi in conversation with the author.
6. *Newsweek*, 16 November 1987.
7. Ben Yahia in conversation with the author.

8. Hermassi in conversation with the author.

9. Chaabane, *Ben Ali*, pp. 20–21.

10. Ibid.

11. U.S. diplomatic dispatch made available to the author.

12. Michael C. Dunn, *Renaissance or Radicalism? Political Islam: The Case of Tunisia's al-Nahda* (Washington, D.C.: International Estimate, 1992), p. vii.

13. Hedi Mechri in conversation with the author.

14. *Le Monde Diplomatique*, July 1996.

15. Dunn, *Renaissance or Radicalism?*, p. viii.

CHAPTER 2

From Hannibal to Bourguiba

Civilizations have come and gone, leaving their relics layer upon layer in the Tunisian soil. Their richness has astounded generations of archaeologists and other scientists who have found the country to be an incredible repository of human ingenuity that testifies to mankind's enterprise and love of art as well as to its stubbornness, greed, cruelty, and pioneering spirit over three millennia.

Founded about 814 B.C. by the Phoenicians, those brilliant traders and colonizers, in its time Carthage ruled most of the known Western world; its merchant ships and men-of-war plyed the Mare Nostrum in every conceivable direction. Legend attributes its founding to "Princess Dido," sister of the king of Tyre. Hannibal with his cohorts and war elephants embarked from its small port for the conquest of Rome, crossing the Alps in an epic march and casting fear across the peninsula as the cry *"Hannibal ante portas"*—Hannibal before the gates—heralded carnage. The Carthaginians built cities and trading posts around the Mediterranean, which the Romans were to inherit—and destroy. The Carthaginian era continues to fascinate researchers to this day, but the only documents preserved of that period were written by Romans themselves pledged to the destruction of Carthage's power.

It was a period when mercy was rare and cruelty refined. Children were sacrificed to the gods Baal, Eshmun, and Tanit. Military commanders were crucified for failure by Carthaginians, whom Roman chroniclers described as "cruel, cowardly, lecherous and over-ambitious." During the "Revolt of the Mercenaries" in 237 B.C., some 40,000 rebellious Berber soldiers were trampled to death by elephants. Today's inhabitants of Carthage, a mani-cured, palm-shaded suburb of Tunis and also the seat of its present-day took place right there, where the blue Mediterranean enters the bay of Tunis. Some 600,000 Carthaginians died of hunger or in fierce combat as Roman legions fought to destroy their city. When it finally fell, gutted by fire and littered with piles of corpses, Scipio the Africanus, the victorious com-mander, ordered the ruins leveled, and "the land then ploughed over and sown with salt to make it barren."

Other cities built by Carthaginians were scattered throughout Tunisia: Dougga, Bulla, Thuburbo Maius—to name a few. All were eventually settled by Romans, who, having subdued Berber kings, decided on a more peaceful and constructive existence. The mosaics, statues, and other relics admired by millions of tourists today are mostly of Roman origin. During that period the area known today as Tunisia did not have to be policed by massive garrisons. The only military presence was in the form of the famous "Third Legion Augusta," stationed near what today is the Algerian border. Tunisia was Rome's "African province," soon to be Arabized into "Ifriquiya."

As this study is mainly concerned with modern-day Tunisia, it would be impractical to try to recall even a small part of the fascinating events of its ancient history. Hundreds of learned historians have done it over the years, and this work is mainly intended to highlight that which inspired today's Tunisians to seek their beginnings while embracing all ethnic groups under the slogan "we are all Carthaginians." Because all major religions of Europe, Africa, and the Middle East had a role in shaping the country which became perhaps the first melting pot of the area, "receptive to the trade winds and the crosscurrents of Mediterranean civilization."[1]

Tunisia's original inhabitants were Berbers, the name derived from the Roman "barbari"—barbarian or uncouth—which somehow stuck through-out the centuries. Nomadic, or semi-nomadic, the Berbers were led by kings who made an impact on history: Massinissa, Jugurtha, and Juba, to mention a few. In the 7th century, Arabs from what today is Egypt started raiding North Africa in search of loot. According to Ibn Khaldoun, traveler, writer and perhaps the greatest historian of early Arab conquests, the Arabs "set out to propagate their religion among other nations. Their armies pene-trated into the Maghreb and captured all its camps and cities."[2]

In the year 670, Ukbah ibn Nafi set out from Egypt at the head of Arab armies and led them into the heart of Tunisia, founding his capital at Kairouan, promising to "build a city which can serve as a place of arms for Islam until the end of time." The construction of Kairouan's Great Mosque began and was to last five years. Kairouan became the base of further Arab conquest in North Africa and a major religious center of Islam. In the 9th century A.D., a dynasty founded by Ibrahim ibn Aghlab, who headed a tribe subsequently known as the Aghlabites, made Kairouan Tunisia's capital. It was destroyed in 1057, only to be rebuilt later—the fate of most famous cities in North Africa.

Christianity, which had followed the Roman and Vandal conquests, settled in Tunisia to some extent, until it was deposed from its ornate throne by Islam. In a way, it survived as a major factor until the end of the French colonial rule. "The Muslim invasion of North Africa wiped out the Christian presence here," Bourguiba told John Cooley, correspondent of the *Christian Science Monitor* in 1962.

Since then, I regret to say, the Christians have always been associated with colonizers. The Christians, down through our history, have always wanted to evangelize, to Christianize, and to re-Christianize North Africa.

The future of the Roman Church, of the churches, in North Africa? It will be about the same as that of the Europeans themselves. On the day when the last remnants of colonialism are gone, our relations with the Christian church will be exemplary and ideal.[3]

Obviously, the reduction of the Christian community to a few thousand throughout the Maghreb facilitated this "exemplary" relationship, reflecting, to some extent, the old president's prophetic vision of the post-colonial world.

Early in the millennium, Tunisia was in the path of the knights bearing the cross in their efforts to wrest Jerusalem from the Muslims. King Louis IX of France set off for Tunisia in 1270, presumably to use it as the major staging area for the last crusade. He landed unopposed on July 18 with 6,000 knights and 30,000 foot soldiers, and shortly thereafter the ruling sultan Al-Mustansir proclaimed a *jihad* or holy war throughout North Africa. From various parts of Tunisia, from Algeria and from as far as Morocco, Berber armies converged to fight for the cause of Islam, backed by doctors of law and Islamic clerics. Although the Christians initially held their ground, the death of King Louis IX of fever turned the tide in favor of the sultan and of a negotiated truce. As the remnants of the Christian expedition sailed back to France, a freak Mediterranean storm sank some of their ships and damaged the others. The Muslims regarded this mishap as a clear sign from God.

That, of course, was not the end of Christianity near the Roman ruins of Carthage. Various Christian settlements followed, including the Andalusians and the Knights of St. John, who established a vast and lucrative trade in slaves. To this day, on the hill rising above the residential suburb and the presidential palace, is the cathedral built after the French protectorate was established in 1881. The cathedral no longer serves as a house of God, and the nearby monastery, once the home of the White Fathers of Africa, is now a museum with a magnificent collection of artifacts. The Carthage congregation of mostly foreign residents has diminished to a few hundred, and not all of them are practicing Catholics. As Bourguiba said, relations between Islam and catholicism after the end of colonialism have become "exemplary."

During the 16th century, Tunisia was the scene of many confrontations between Ottoman Turkey and the Christian powers. After several bloody battles and other vicissitudes, the Sublime Porte (Istanbul) triumphed in 1574. Ottoman Turks began to rule Tunisia and other parts of North Africa and were periodically challenged by military revolts. In 1702, a rebellion by Hussein bin Ali installed a dynasty of "beys" called the Husseinites, which was to survive until a year after Tunisia's independence.

The Ottoman Turks, ruling from Istanbul, applied their traditional pattern of colonization by appointing "delegates" whose job was to keep the provinces under control and, above all, collect taxes. Such a system in the Turkish possessions continued virtually until the end of the Ottoman empire in the 20th century. While supplying the Sublime Porte with a flow of cash and, frequently, troops for various wars, the Turkish colonial period left no lasting heritage across North Africa, southeastern Europe, or the Middle East, the exception being the Turks' highly appreciated art of cooking. In some areas, particularly in the Middle East and in Greece, the Ottoman empire left behind considerable rancor and bitterness of a ruthless rule and of cruel punishment.

Initially, Tunisia was ruled by a *pasha* who worked closely with the colonial military establishment. Eventually "beys" became the highest ranking officials in the Tunisian province, which occupied roughly the same territory as it does today. The beys varied from benign to ruthless, and some employed fleets of pirate ships to criss-cross the nearby waters of the Mediterranean, attacking and plundering the merchant vessels of the European powers. The long period of Turkish rule witnessed the building of some of Tunisia's most stunning mosques, as well as palaces and other princely dwellings. Tunisia in those days was dotted, as it is today, with ancient *ribats*, or fortresses, and some remnants of the Andalusian period as well as with often-spectacular vestiges of the Roman era, including the El Djem coliseum, Dougga, the remains of an aqueduct that used to link Zaghouane with Tunis, and myriad others.

Washed by the Mediterranean from the north and along the eastern coast, it stretched southward into the Sahara, then a daunting barrier, and a challenge to explorers and traders. In the northwest, lush green mountain forests separated it from Algeria, also ruled by the revenue-hungry Sublime Porte.

Modern-age historians tend to believe that, although a colony of the Ottomans, Tunisia functioned by "taking its distance from the Ottoman empire." According to Noureddine Dougui, head of the Institut Supérieur d'Histoire du Mouvement National in Tunis, "the bey collected taxes, considered the Ottomans as spiritual leaders (of Islam) and recognized the sultan as the caliph (successor of the Prophet) and commander of the believers."[4]

In those days, Friday's Muslim prayers were conducted in the name of the sultan. The coins in circulation at the beginning of the 19th century had the sultan's likeness on one side and Tunisia's coat of arms on the other. Troops had to be provided whenever the sultan demanded. Thus, for example, during the Crimean War in 1854, Tunisia dispatched a contingent, which fought under the Tunisian flag and a Tunisian commander, on the side of the Ottoman troops. In a way, although a vassal of the Turkish empire, Tunisia had "its own personality."[5]

The struggle among European powers for influence in North Africa and generally along the southern coast of the Mediterranean intensified after the French conquest of Algeria in 1830. Along with the French expeditionary force came priests and missionaries, some of whom, although constricted by the secular government in Paris, attempted to re-Christianize the area. The most prominent among them was Cardinal Charles Lavigerie who firmly believed it was France's "duty" to proselytize. Although "the last prominent defender of the crusading and royalist tradition in religion, government and politics,"[6] Lavigerie made little impact on Tunisia, even after the establishment of both the French protectorate and a Catholic diocese of Tunis, which was subsequently turned into an archdiocese and moved to Carthage. Eventually, he focused his attention on converting the mainly animist areas of sub-Sahara Africa.

Religion had little to do with the struggle for political and commercial influence which then unfolded in the area and mainly pitted France against Italy. Tunisia's ruler during that crucial period in the country's history was Mohammed es-Saddok (1859–1882), who is remembered in Tunisian history as the man who granted the country its first constitution, in 1861. It was, by the prevailing standards, an extremely liberal document and to this day Tunisians call it the first constitution in the Arabo-Muslim world.

The document (unfortunately later ignored when Tunisia became a protectorate of France) guaranteed civil and religious liberties, established a responsible ministry and the separation of powers along the lines of other such charters existing in Europe at the time. It limited the bey's powers and, in effect, set up a constitutional monarchy. Historians debate whether the constitution, imposed by the combined pressures of France, Italy, and Great Britain, was too advanced for the population of Tunisia, particularly since it caused a religious revolt. But the Arabic term *destour*, or constitution, remained the main guideline and slogan in most political movements struggling for Tunisia's independence, and, subsequently, for its development and democracy. Thus, the Destour Party of the early 1920s later became Neo-Destour, then changed into the Socialist Destour Party, and, most recently into the Constitutional Democratic Rally. The word "constitution" thus became firmly embedded in Tunisia's political tradition.

The adoption of the constitution did not disrupt French plans to expand their North African possessions. Part of their strategy was to press the bey to accept foreign loans that he was incapable of repaying. In simple terms, by 1869, the official ruler of Tunisia was deeply in debt—mainly to French banks and companies. The situation was such that bankruptcy was officially declared, and an international commission was set up to administer Tunisia's finances and exact its debt payments. The commission was presided over by a Frenchman. For all intents and purposes, Tunisia had lost its independence.

In 1881, using Berber raids from Tunisia into Algerian territory as a pretext, French troops from Algeria entered Tunisia by land and by sea. After some resistance by Berber tribes, on May 12 of that year the "Treaty of Bardo" (or *Kasr-es-Said*) was signed, giving France the right to occupy Tunisian territory until "order was re-established," to control its foreign relations and to supervise its finances. Officially, Tunisia became a protectorate. In effect, it was a buffer with which the French government intended to protect the eastern flank of its Algerian territory. In 1883, a further step was taken by a convention under which France was to appoint a "resident general" and advisers in virtually all Tunisian affairs.

While neighboring Algeria was, at least theoretically, a portion of France, Tunisia was a protectorate which recognized the Tunisian state. France was pledged to "defend the throne" of the bey, whose power was progressively "emptied of substance."[7] There was a Tunisian prime minister and a cabinet of 12 ministers—only two of whom were Tunisians. The bey's power consisted mainly of signing decrees—submitted to him by Frenchmen. France paid for its troops stationed in Tunisia, but everything else was paid for by taxes collected from the Tunisian population. In effect, its presence in Tunisia cost France nothing.

The early period of the protectorate was accompanied by the arrival of French civil servants and administrators whose pay included what was known as *le tiers colonial*—literally a "colonial third"—meaning they were paid one third more than Tunisians doing the same jobs. This, inevitably, created two classes of citizens, and Tunisians complained that their country was becoming "a colony of civil servants."

Genuine settlers known as "colons" arrived later, when the protectorate authorities passed a law in effect nationalizing the land belonging to the bey. The measure also included all land without specific title deeds. Thus, the protectorate took over some 800,000 hectares (nearly two million acres) in the most fertile parts of Tunisia, subsequently sold, for pathetically symbolic sums, to Frenchmen willing to settle and work in France's latest colonial acquisition. The "colons" constructed sturdy farms and generally acquired a comfortable existence in sharp contrast to that of the indigenous population. By the turn of the century, the disproportion in the standard of living, according to Tunisian figures, was enormous: while all French children went to school, only between 7 percent and 8 percent of Tunisian children had access to primary education. The colonization was accompanied by the construction of Catholic churches throughout the country although, at least in theory, Tunisia still owed allegiance to Muslim Turkey.

At the same time, however, the protectorate authorities launched a program of training Tunisian policemen and teachers, not only for Arabic education but also for subjects taught in French. This trend continued throughout the colonial period, providing Tunisia with experienced administrators and an educated elite, an enormous asset when independence came in 1956. And it was this elite that began to demand greater freedom, initially in the form of autonomy, and formed a political movement that eventually led to the creation of the Destour (constitution), Tunisia's first political party.

The press organ of those young Tunisian intellectuals was *Le Jeune Tunisien*, an increasingly vocal newspaper demanding equal rights and autonomy in a country dominated by the French colonial power. It was clear that nationalism had begun to grow in Tunisia, whose predominantly Islamic population was stirred by the Italian invasion of nearby Tripolitania. A dispute about plans to build a road across the Muslim El Djellez cemetery in Tunis caused a mass demonstration in 1911 which resulted in the first confrontation between Tunisians and French colonial troops. There were dead and wounded on both sides. In February 1912, a tram driven by an Italian settler hit a Tunisian child and caused a Tunisian boycott of the line. *Le Jeune Tunisien* formed a support committee, an act to which the authorities reacted by shutting it down. The leaders of the boycott were arrested and some were exiled. To continue their anti-colonial political activity, a number of young Tunisians went into exile, mainly to Switzerland and Turkey.

The outbreak of World War I interrupted Tunisian political activities. Some 60,000 Tunisians were mobilized and sent to the trenches to fight for France. The end of the war and President Woodrow Wilson's "14 points" electrified Tunisian nationalists again. In his book *La Tunisie Martyre*, Abdelaziz Thaalbi bluntly denounces the excesses and abuses of the protectorate. The book was subsequently regarded by Tunisian historians as a "veritable manifesto of Tunisian nationalism."[8] Thaalbi's message was simple: Tunisians should fully participate in running their own country. However, his manifesto stopped short of calling for outright independence. Such a cautious, gradual, and exceptionally pragmatic approach was to characterize Tunisian nationalists in years to come. It facilitated Tunisia's subsequent struggle for independence with a minimum of victims.

In 1920 Thaalbi founded the Destour Party, with backing from some ulema (Muslim scholars) of the famous Islamic Zitouna University in Tunis, as well as those in Kairouan. The party's 9-point program basically called for a real constitution, considering the one adopted in 1861 as an outdated and useless charter de facto superseded by the protectorate. Its value lay in the fact that it was the first such document in Arab history. The time had come for young, educated Tunisians to demand concessions from the protectorate, a process which lasted for half a century.

Incidents and repression intensified in the early 1920s. Under strong pressure from the nationalists, the bey, a mere figurehead at best, accepted the Destour program in 1922.

The face of Tunisia had changed considerably from the days when its harbors sheltered pirates and the first European traders arrived in search of such bargains as Tunisian olive oil, dates, and spices. European quarters sprang up next to the *medinas*, or old cities, whose labyrinths of narrow streets were lined with small houses usually painted white with blue shutters and crowded *souks* (markets) where one could buy exquisitely woven carpets from Kairouan and silver bracelets engraved with elaborate Arabic writing. Tunisian ports, particularly Tunis, Bizerta, Sfax and Sousse, became cosmopolitan trading centers, where Arabs, Europeans, Jews, and Maltese rubbed shoulders and concluded deals over tiny cups of scented coffee. Next to the medinas, the colonizers erected their own cities graced with broad palm-lined streets and shops and cafes where the colonial elite could lead its separate life. The Tunisian world existed apart; to Europeans it was a strange Oriental world of women clutching white *haiks* to their faces and men increasingly wearing European suits with red fezzes rakishly tilted on their heads. The two worlds co-existed but rarely mixed, although as time went by more and more Tunisians spoke French and adopted European ways and inter-marriage became more frequent, particularly between educated Tunisian men and French women.

Jews from Italy had settled in large numbers. In addition, Tunisia was home to the ancient and assimilated Jewish community which started on the southern island of Djerba. These indigenous Jews spoke Arabic and tended to group together in such areas as the port of La Goulette outside Tunis, and in a number of others areas. According to Dr. Gabriel Kabla, a Djerba-born Jewish activist now living in France, "we were here (in Tunisia) before the Bible. There isn't a square yard of Tunisia which has not been marked by Judaism."[9] The latest arrivals of Jews were mainly from the Italian city of Livorno (Leghorn) and, while adopting the French language, usually held Italian citizenship and tended to look to Italy. In the period preceding World War II, that part of the Jewish community was an important asset in fascist Italy's posturing in the area.

Amidst the colorful and cosmopolitan setting of Tunisia of the 1920s, the Destour Party began to make serious inroads in society. Its organizational structure expanded from the cities into the countryside, and, by about 1925, the party had between 30,000 to 40,000 card-carrying members. Still, its activities in 1924 were overshadowed by the formation of the Tunisian General Workers Union (*Union Générale de Travailleurs Tunisiens*—UGTT) by

Mohammed Ali, a pioneering experience in the history of organized labor in the Arab world. Destour waited, while Tunisia was in the throes of an economic crisis which went on well into the 1930s. Ironically, while a large part of the population starved, the French marked the 100th anniversary of Algeria's conquest in 1931 with panache and even extravagance. Such a form of colonial insouciance only helped fuel the nascent Tunisian nationalism, by then grouped around another French language publication, "*L'Action Tunisienne*," which attracted some of the best talent in the country. Among its contributors was a young nationalist with strongly secular views who was to become Tunisia's first president, Habib Bourguiba.

During the 1930s, Tunisia became the object of considerable foreign interest and competition, given its strategic position and several easily accessible seaports. France's key competitor was Mussolini's Italy, presumably intent on extending its influence over the nearby French protectorate from its base in Libya. The presence of a large Italian colony in Tunisia, which eventually reached some 120,000 people, was an unquestionable asset in Italy's policies. Some Tunisian historians estimate the number of Italians higher because many did not have residence documents and were not registered with the Italian consulate. The consulate itself was the center of intense Italian activity—a sort of "fifth column" against the protectorate. At that time Tunisia's French population was estimated at about 80,000. (Following a brief German occupation during World War II, there was considerable "settling of accounts" with local Italians when the French administration returned in 1943. A number of Italians were considered by the French to be pro-Nazi collaborators.)

The rise of fascism in Italy, and particularly in Germany in the middle 1930s, prompted the protectorate authorities to adopt some form of appeasement toward Tunisian nationalists. But the project which the French considered to be the most tantalizing, that of Tunisians' "naturalization," had the opposite effect. Tunisian nationalists did not want to lose their identity and thus opposed the idea, which was soon shelved.

Meanwhile, the nationalists had to face a crisis of ideas of their own, leading to the breakup of the Destour Party. A party congress at Ksar Hellal in 1934 formally approved the split, with the "old" traditional wing, headed by Thaalbi, keeping the name and the rebels becoming Neo-Destour, governed by a Political Bureau chaired by Mahmoud Matri and with Bourguiba as secretary general.

Those were the days of fiery orators—including Bourguiba—who relentlessly toured the countryside, stirring up Tunisia's political awareness. The habit stayed with Bourguiba after independence as he delivered rambling speeches on the radio, often repetitious and almost never from a prepared text.

Inevitably, the activities and growing strength of Tunisian nationalists alarmed the protectorate authorities. In September 1934, the French resident general decided to have the key leaders arrested and deported to the desert. Rioting broke out in parts of Tunisia and troops intervened. There were dead and wounded. When the Socialist Popular Front came to power in France in 1936, Premier Leon Blum revoked the order. But Tunisia's quietude did not last long as the clouds of war gathered over Europe. When pro-nationalist mass demonstrations took place on April 9, 1938, the French authorities clamped a state of siege on the country. Troops patrolled the streets; there were victims. The two wings of Destour were banned, and members of the Political Bureau were thrown in jail. The ban persisted until 1954, when France granted internal autonomy to its protectorate.

The nationalists did not, however, disarm and continued waging a campaign of tracts and other forms of political activity, albeit at a reduced scale. German troops landed in Tunisia in November 1942, apparently believing that a large bridgehead around Tunis and Bizerta could be established and held, thus tying up the Allied armies advancing from the south. On March 5, 1943, Field Marshal Erwin Rommel fought his last battle on Tunisian soil, at Medenine. A week later he left for Germany, admitting that "in the long run neither Libya nor Tunisia could have been held, for the African war was decided by the battle of the Atlantic."[10]

Bourguiba spent the war in prison, first in France and subsequently in Italy, but maintained contact with Habib Thameur, a Destour official working clandestinely in Tunisia. Above all, Bourguiba warned Thameur not to collaborate with the Germans, although personally he believed that it was not Tunisia's war. Still, as long as hostilities lasted, Bourguiba did not want to pressure the colonial authorities in any way, using his traditionally cautious approach.

In 1945, Bourguiba went to Cairo, and his long-time rival, Salah Ben Youssef, took control of the Destour movement. An energetic organizer, frequently dogmatic, he advocated immediate independence rather than Bourguiba's policy of gradual reforms and internal autonomy as an intermediate stage. While Bourguiba believed in modernism and a Western-type society, Ben Youssef was inclined toward traditionalism. Years later, Abdelaziz Ben Dhia, secretary general of the Constitutional Democratic Rally which replaced Neo-Destour after Ben Ali's takeover, recalled that "there was a considerable clash of personalities," in the party.[11]

In August 1946, the party held what has become known as "a congress of independence," during which various factions agreed to forget their quarrels and passed a motion demanding abolition of the protectorate, sovereignty for Tunisia, and membership in the United Nations and the Arab League. Although police raided the congress and arrested some 300 participants, it was obvious that the French authorities were facing a serious challenge. Tunisian nationalism was on the warpath; the march toward independence had begun in earnest.

Realizing the extent of the challenge, the French admitted the need for reforms, at the same time hoping that various half-measures would satisfy the nationalists, at least in the immediate future. Consequently, the number of Tunisians in the 12–man cabinet was increased from two to six. But in 1950, a new resident general, Louis Perrier, warned the Tunisians from the beginning that no dramatic changes should be expected. Shortly afterward, Premier Robert Schuman made a speech interpreted by Tunisians as "no" to independence.

Salah Ben Youssef, Bourguiba's rival, was by then in the cabinet as minister of justice and continued pushing for independence, while the other Tunisian ministers talked of the need for "stages" (*étapes*). On the other hand, the government in Paris was under considerable pressure from French settlers in Tunisia (by then some 180,000) to resist Tunisian nationalists at all costs. In a note of December 15, 1951, Schuman proposed a scheme, which he called "double sovereignty," between France and Tunisia, which stated that Frenchmen would continue governing the country— anathema to all Tunisian nationalist factions.

Armed resistance broke out in parts of Tunisia in January 1952. A new French resident general arrived, this time aboard a warship which docked at the French naval base of Bizerta. Bourguiba was arrested for the third time. French settlers in the countryside were fortifying their farms and amassing weapons. Some later joined a shadowy organization known as "the Red Hand," which answered nationalist attacks with a terrorist campaign of its own. The nascent Tunisian guerrilla movement attacked military and strategic objectives as well as some French farms. There was no structured general command, but most groups looked up to Neo-Destour. A climate of insecurity reigned in large portions of Tunisia.

By 1954, French Premier Pierre Mendes-France decided that Algeria was France's priority and, if necessary, Tunisia could be allowed to go its separate way. In a speech in Carthage on July 31, 1954, Mendes-France outlined the principle of internal autonomy. Soon after, on November 1, 1954 a revolt against French rule broke out in eastern Algeria and spread throughout the country, eventually tying up half a million French troops. Algeria, with its million French settlers and newly discovered oilfields at Hassi Messaoud, became France's main worry in North Africa for seven tortuous years. The war raging beyond its western frontier also marred Tunisia's first years of independence and harmed its relationship with France.

On July 1, 1955, Bourguiba returned to Tunis after years of imprisonment and exile, cheered by massive crowds gathered in the port of La Goulette. He was a national hero, vindicated and triumphant. An agreement on Tunisia's autonomy was signed two days later. In November of that year, Neo-Destour held a congress in the southern city of Sfax, which disavowed

Ben Youssef. Bourguiba triumphed again and became "father of the nation," which formally became independent on March 20, 1956.

NOTES

1. John K. Cooley, *Baal, Christ, and Mohammed: Religion and Revolution in North Africa* (New York: Holt, Rinehart and Winston, 1965), p. 193.

2. Ibn Khaldoun, *Prolegomena* (Paris, 1934).

3. Cooley, Baal, Christ, and Mohammed, pp. 3–4.

4. Noureddine Dougui in conversation with the author.

5. Ibid.

6. Cooley, Baal, Christ, and Mohammed, p. 222.

7. Noureddine Dougui in conversation with the author.

8. Ibid.

9. Gabriel Kabla in conversation with the author.

10. Desmond Young, *Rommel, The Desert Fox* (New York: Harper, 1950), p. 255.

11. Abdelaziz Ben Dhia in conversation with the author.

CHAPTER 3

The Supreme Warrior

Once the bright lights of festivities were extinguished, to many Tunisians independence seemed a bit of an anti-climax. After all, over ten months before, they had all shouted *Yahia Bourguiba* (long live Bourguiba) when the "Supreme Warrior" descended from his ship at La Goulette after years of imprisonment and forced exile. They had applauded when Ben Youssef was disavowed at the party congress in November and when, during the following months, French colonial dignitaries started packing their belongings in their seaside villas and official residences to make room for a new ruling class. They had watched with bemusement—and perhaps with some emotional pangs—the last public *prises d'armes* (military ceremonies around the French tricolor) in which the colonial army excelled. All this was the result of a long, arduous struggle and perseverance, carefully crafted and guided by all those who believed in Bourguiba and his tactics, marked by caution and determination, a seemingly strange but obviously effective combination.

Meanwhile, next door, Algeria was on fire, and every day new ships disembarked more French troops and war materiel. And Tunisia was to pay part of the price for the French determination to resist Algerian nationalism—while recognizing that of Morocco and Tunisia.

For Bourguiba, the "long march" was finished and a new chapter, perhaps even more difficult, was beginning. A French-trained lawyer and intellectual, a man who could recite Arabic poems along with those of La Fontaine and Verlaine and plunge with gusto into erudite discussions on ephemeral subjects in either of the two languages, Bourguiba wanted to be both an Arab and a cosmopolitan. Small and compact, he paid a lot of attention to his attire and preferred dark, sometimes striped, suits. He knew the power of his extraordinary blue eyes. Foreign visitors were frequently seduced by his charm. While Ataturk loved his feet and frequently padded around barefoot while receiving his foreign guests, Bourguiba loved all of himself. Small wonder that, as time went by, he increased national veneration of his person and of his achievements. Politically, he was tempted by French-style liberalism and, at the same time, by what he liked to describe as "controlled democracy."[1] The latter concept seems to have prevailed for years after Tunisia's independence. In any case, Bourguiba now had a forum and an admiring nation all to himself—except for the shadow of Ben Youssef over parts of the Tunisian south. From his Egyptian exile, le Djerbien (Ben Youssef was born on the island of Djerba) continued to harass, verbally, the head of liberated Tunisia, for no apparent reason, calling him a traitor. Bourguiba's most fierce opponent was found dead in a Munich hotel room in 1961.

Although this book is not about Bourguiba but about modern-age Tunisia, it would be impossible to limit the part dealing with the personality of its first post-independence leader. For more than 30 years, to many Tunisians, Bourguiba and Tunisia were inseparable. He was responsible for Tunisia's successes and failures because he alone bore the responsibility for the system of the country's "controlled democracy." Hence, limiting or skirting parts dealing with his impact on Tunisia would be historically misleading. Bourguiba's successors understood perfectly the meaning, the importance, and the role of the old "Supreme Warrior." Streets named after the first president remained unchanged for years, and no statues of Bourguiba were knocked off their socles after the 1987 Change. As late as March 1997, Ben Ali visited the "grand monsieur" in his secluded residence of Monastir, where he had been born, and by doing so acknowledged the old man's importance to modern Tunisia. Many of Bourguiba's critics in Tunisia admitted years after his removal that perhaps his greatest fault was not to have abandoned power earlier.

In the months following its independence, Tunisia was in limbo. While the French administrators had prepared for the inevitable departure, the settlers waited, uncertain of the new nation's future policies. It was obvious that, sooner or later, the country was going to be "Tunisified," and that new Tunisian elites would replace the French, Jews, Italians, and Maltese of yesteryear. A sizeable French military contingent remained in Tunisia, and the French navy kept control of the large naval base at Bizerta. A new Tunisian administration was making its first tentative steps and during the first years all government departments used the French language. Six years after independence only two ministries—defense and interior—were fully "Arabized." The others did not even have Arabic typewriters or people able to use them.

Most government offices in Tunis were located in the so-called Casbah overlooking the medina (old city) with its minarets, mysteries, and scent of spices. Some office buildings were in the elaborate Moorish style, with exquisite tiles and hand-woven carpets. Along the nearby Bab Benat boulevard, "public writers" advertized their trade next to hole-in-the-wall cafes selling *merguez* (spicy lamb sausages) and other Tunisian specialties. Lawyers did brisk business in adjacent courts.

Hotels in the center of the city still had mostly European staffs, and one could see French soldiers in their blue *kepis*, or forage caps, strolling along the tree-lined central thoroughfare, Avenue Jules Ferry, soon to bear Bourguiba's name.

The new state was poor, even very poor. Of its 3.7 million inhabitants, the rural population constituted 67 percent. The average life expectancy was 50 years. There were only 548 medical doctors in the country, most of them Europeans. Only 23 percent of Tunisian children went to school, and the galloping birthrate stood at 51 per 1000. The per capita income was about $100 per year, estimated in today's terms at about $500.

As French and Italian settlers started to leave the country, Tunisia discovered a paucity of trained economists and heads of enterprises. Thus the state had to take charge of the economy, a move that was necessary but weighed over Tunisia's development for years to come. Tunisia did have a large class of lower- and middle-level civil servants who turned out to be an enormous asset during the difficult transition period. The increasing encroachment of the state in the economy was "not a question of ideology or doctrine but of necessity."[2]

Reforms of the state and political structure took place gradually. On July 25, 1957, Bourguiba, who was then prime minister, together with the parliament dominated by the ruling Neo-Destour Party, formally dethroned Lamine Bey, the 19th and last bey of Tunis. With the monarchy thus abolished, Tunisia officially became a republic following adoption of its constitution on June 1, 1959, which describes Tunisia as a state whose religion is Islam, whose language Arabic, and which "constitutes a part of the Greater Maghreb, for the unity of which it works in the common interest." (The concept of "Greater Maghreb" comprises Libya, Tunisia, Algeria, Morocco, and Mauritania. At the time of the adoption of the Tunisian constitution, Algeria was officially a part of France and Mauritania was still a French colony.)

The constitution guarantees "the dignity of the individual and liberty of conscience and protects the free exercise of religions, on condition that they do not disturb public order." The charter reserved the office of the president for a Muslim, and Bourguiba, the only candidate, was elected with the participation of 91 percent of registered voters in November 1959.

The year of Tunisia's independence was filled with trepidation. In July, Egyptian President Gamal Abdel Nasser nationalized the Suez Canal, prompting France and Great Britain to launch a naval and airborne attack on Port Said in November to wrest control of the waterway, an action stopped in midstream by U.S. pressure and Soviet threats.

The Suez Canal operation and its aftermath had long-lasting repercussions in Europe, the Middle East, and, indeed, in the entire Arab world. It demonstrated Western Europe's vulnerability in the face of such precarious oil routes as the Suez Canal and Nasser's ability to turn defeat into victory. France's accusations that Egypt was a de facto co-belligerent in the Algerian war had no impact on the unfolding situation.

While French paratroopers of the 10th Division flying from the then British colony of Cyprus secured Port Fuad and their British colleagues dropped on Port Said, in the central part of the strategic canal the Israelis seized the road to Ismailia after their armor knifed across the Sinai in an epic desert blitz. The world looked with awe at newsreel pictures of thousands of abandoned Egyptian tanks and other vehicles, while in Cairo Nasser trumpeted victory. The Arab world believed him and not without reason: President Dwight D. Eisenhower formally announced that Washington had not been consulted, did not believe in the use of force, and did not intend to become involved in the war. The Soviet government served notice that it was prepared to use force to stop the Anglo-French "Operation Telescope." The French advance southward of Port Said was thwarted. Embittered paratroopers, still smarting from defeat in Indochina, returned to Algeria and were regarded by the Algerian rebels as the losers of yet another war. The Algerian nationalists soon launched what has become known as "the battle of Algiers," a massive and indiscriminate wave of terror, mainly against European settlers.

But Nasser triumphed: Egypt kept control of the canal while Western Europe shivered during the long winter months as oil tankers were rerouted around Africa before sunken ships could all be removed to open the waterway to navigation again. The Israelis pulled back to their besieged country. The 1956 sweep across the Sinai was a prelude to a similar blitz 11 years later, during the so-called "six-day war" in 1967. But even that action did not shake Nasser. There was no one to rival him in the Arab world.

In the fall of 1956, as storm clouds were gathering over the Suez Canal, the Arabs were confronted by another significant event that was to damage their relations with France. On October 24, a plane carrying five leaders of the Algerian nationalist movement from Morocco to Tunis was intercepted, with the pilot's complicity, by the French and taken to Algiers. The five, including future president Ahmed Ben Bella, spent the rest of the war in prison. Arab passions ran high, and Bourguiba felt he should act like an Arab. Tunisia's relations with France plunged to rock-bottom depths, particularly as, by then, the Algerian *Front de Libération Nationale* (FLN) was openly using Tunisia as its major external base. Algerian rebel envoys frequently traveled with Tunisian passports, and FLN camps were established along the Algerian border in Tunisia, from where men, arms, and supplies poured into Algeria. Such a situation prompted the French to build a highly fortified and electrified defense line along their side of the frontier, the so-called "Ligne Morice," named after André Morice, a defense minister.

Bourguiba's reactions in those days were often impulsive and even provocative. He had obtained independence for his country, but his freedom of action was limited by Tunisia's poverty and the rather unceremonious behavior of the FLN on Tunisian soil. Bourguiba felt he had little choice, because the Algerians were "brothers" engaged in a fight for independence. Some Tunisians did not have such strong feelings, and many resented the encroachment by the Algerian politico-military apparatus on their home ground.

Exacerbating Bourguiba's problem was the continuing French military presence in Tunisia. At one stage of the war of nerves between Tunisia and France, Bourguiba called on the population to "build trenches," although it was not clear why. Another time he ordered a "freeze" on the movement of all French military personnel that was to last three days. (It was said that 143 French soldiers were caught by the "freeze" in the bawdy houses of Tunis.) The most serious incident, which put additional strain on the relations between the two countries, took place on February 8, 1958, when French bombers raided the town of Sakiet Sidi Youssef, near the border with Algeria, on a market day, killing scores of people. France claimed the town was one of the main supply centers of the Algerian rebellion; the Tunisians denied it. It was clear the two countries no longer agreed on anything.

Despite such vicissitudes, Bourguiba plodded on with reforms putting into being his vision of a modern, progressive Tunisia. By standards prevailing in the Arab world, some of his actions were revolutionary. They included the granting of equal status to women, an intensive fight against illiteracy, a campaign for birth control to reduce the threatening population explosion, and even a scheme to put the unemployed on road construction projects. A German development company started constructing the first hotel on the island of Djerba, the first tangible sign of Tunisia's future as a major tourist attraction.

On May 13, 1958, amidst vacillation by the constantly changing governments of the moribund French Fourth Republic, French settlers in Algeria revolted in the name of their slogan of *Algérie Française*. The rebellion, accompanied by an organized mob attack on the building of the "gouvernement général" in Algiers, was almost immediately joined by the command of the French army, or at least by the headquarters of its 10th Military Region nearby. Officially, the generals explained their act as an effort to control the potentially destabilizing revolt. In effect, the military involvement was clearly exploited by partisans of General Charles de Gaulle to facilitate his return to power.

De Gaulle perfectly understood the Algerian problem and its devastating impact on France and on France's collapsing overseas empire. But given the deep and emotional commitment of the army to defend the French presence in Algeria, he could only try different approaches which, inevitably, failed. The Algerian rebels immediately—and brilliantly—analyzed de Gaulle's strategy and refused various half-hearted offers and measures. Thus the war continued for four more years, damaging France's international reputation and also its relations with Tunisia.

Another event that further eroded Bourguiba's difficult dialogue with Paris was the formation, on September 19, 1958, of the "Provisional Government of the Algerian Republic" (GPRA) by the FLN in Tunis. It was the 1,416th day of the Algerian revolt, and Tunisia became host to this government-in- exile, which attracted a steady stream of journalists to Tunis. The Bourguiba government was a mere side show, and few international newspapers were interested in the plight of Tunisia except as the host to the rebels defying the haughty French president.

Ferhat Abbas, the Algerian "premier," had his headquarters in Tunis and occasionally received journalists in his elegant villa in the Belvedere suburb. M'hammed Yazid, the minister of information, ruled in the decrepit building on the Rue des Entrepreneurs in the heart of the Tunisian capital, where mimeograph machines churned out communiques and Algerian officials were almost as enigmatic as de Gaulle himself.

None of this helped Tunisia and its president, who felt he deserved a better fate than that of a safe haven for Algerians who did know not how to apply his own pragmatic approach to such sensitive problems as independence. Officially, of course, Bourguiba and his government gave wholehearted approval to whatever the Algerians decided to do or not to do. They had little choice.

The Algerians were everywhere. They had their own "military police" roaming Tunis by night and visiting various cafes and nightclubs. Their supplies funded by Egypt and other Arab countries rumbled across Tunisia to such transit points as Le Kef and Ghardimaou. In those areas of western Tunisia, the Algerians seemed perfectly comfortable—and, moreover, were virtually in charge.

The tragedy of the Tunisian population in the border regions was perhaps best summarized by an inhabitant of Ghardimaou, who, pointing to the line of the mountains, said,

obviously, the Algerians are here, in Tunisia, but what can we do? Now and then the French pursue them and we can't really blame them. But we've had enough. The other day the French came with tanks and infantry. Perhaps tomorrow they will send bombers. That's our life: the French on one side, the Algerians on the other and we are stuck in the middle.[3]

In the face of this situation, Bourguiba could only react verbally. Following several major French incursions into Tunisian territory, he announced, in a speech at Teboursouk on April 24, 1960, that "any new attack against our territory or any violation of our airspace will be considered an act of war. . . . We are ready."[4] It was clear, however, that Tunisia was not ready for any armed confrontation with France, which was accusing Tunis of co-belligerence in the Algerian conflict.

As the Algerian war dragged on, and particularly after the failure of the first concrete effort at negotiations in the French spa of Evian-les-Bains in June 1961, Bourguiba became increasingly restless. His wrath centered on the French air and naval base at Bizerta which France simply refused to evacuate, despite various Tunisian diplomatic notes. With Tunisia's economic situation as precarious as ever, Bourguiba decided to create patriotic élan and force the French out of the coastal city some 40 miles north of Tunis. He did not intend to fight but simply to embarrass the French into accepting his demands. In mid-July 1961, several thousand "death volunteers" dressed in blue overalls and carrying obsolete rifles were massed outside the perimeter of the base under the command of Neo-Destour officials. The youths harassed base personnel with slogans under a pall of oppressive summer heat. It was more of a Sunday outing than a siege, but eventually the first shot was fired—no one really knows by whom. The French claimed that Tunisians started lobbing mortar shells into the base. The Tunisians said the French fired first.

The French reaction was swift and brutal. Guns from the base poured fire on parts of Bizerta and on the hapless "death volunteers." Warships of the French Mediterranean fleet headed toward the Tunisian coast. Two paratroop regiments from Algeria, including the crack 2nd Foreign Legion Parachute Regiment (REP), were dropped into the base and quickly expanded the perimeter. After five days of fighting, France and Tunisia agreed to a cease-fire. The French controlled much of the city; their armored cars and jeeps mounting heavy machine guns patroled the debris-strewn streets. The French never bothered to storm the old city known as the Casbah simply because they did not consider it useful from the military point of view and felt such an attack would cause unnecessary casualties.

When the cease-fire came, the Casbah was an armed camp, filled with worn-out civilian volunteers clutching their old Lebel rifles, nurses distributing gauze masks to reduce the stench, and youths manning barricades in the rubble. There was no running water and little food. Houses were being fortified. "Every house will become a fortress," said Youssef Kadouk, head of the local Neo-Destour apparatus.[5] Tunisian losses were estimated at about 1,500 dead, but higher figures were also quoted. To Tunisians, French Admiral Maurice Amman who commanded the base, became "the butcher of Bizerta."

The Tunisian army's role in the clash was minimal, because, despite its peace-keeping service in the Congo (Zaire) it was not combat-ready. Also, Bourguiba had not envisaged such an escalation or the degree of French reaction. By the time various army units reached the embattled city, the French controlled the areas they considered essential to the defense of the installation. A Tunisian artillery unit was smashed by French aircraft as it headed toward the city. Several battalions of Tunisian infantry were deployed in the area, but there was no coherent or organized command. Chaotic orders were simply given by telephone—from Tunis. In the last 36 hours of the fighting, a group of young Tunisian army lieutenants tried to organize some sort of coherent defense, but the French army was firmly in control of a large area around the bases. Warships rode at anchor off the Tunisian coastline.

The months that followed were perhaps the most difficult of the Tunisian president's career. Bourguiba resorted to ordering "protests strikes" by merchants and restaurants, which merely harmed the Tunisians themselves. Dispirited crowds shuffled through Tunis chanting "arms and evacuation." French settlers and Tunisian Jews jammed the docks awaiting ships bound for France. Rents plummeted.

Western diplomats seriously feared that the Bizerta disaster might weaken Bourguiba and create instability. Perhaps influenced by his Western friends, Bourguiba made several conciliatory gestures toward French settlers and political internees arrested during the crisis and signaled to France his willingness to negotiate. Thus the "Supreme Warrior" returned to his traditional policy of moderation and conciliation. Such an about-face received warm, if not enthusiastic, approval from the Tunisian population, most of which showed little support for the Bizerta adventure. Bourguiba never fully explained his motives and his varied reactions. Two weeks after the cease-fire, he described de Gaulle as a die-hard colonialist, as "a man who still lives in the era of the oil lamp and sand clock."[6] In December 1963, the French left Bizerta—at de Gaulle's own timing. Bourguiba celebrated his "victory" together with Presidents Nasser of Egypt and Ben Bella of Algeria. Today almost every Tunisian town has streets named after the "martyrs" (Arabic term for war dead) of the battle of Bizerta.

The departure of many of Tunisia's Jews following the Bizerta crisis was, for a small country, a serious event although at the time the Tunisians were not aware of its impact. The Jews, mostly merchants and members of the professional class, were not leaving for fear of persecution or mob asssault but because they did not have much faith in Tunisia's economic future. Bourguiba's policies at that time were not encouraging for the country's development. Already many of the French enterprises had shut down, and the quasi-socialist policies had a restrictive impact on the economy. Besides, the tensions periodically erupting between Israel and its Arab enemies had, inevitably, affected the security and confidence of Tunisia's Jewish community, which numbered about 110,000 people at the time of the birth of Israel in 1948. Bourguiba's various assurances, although sincere, were taken in the context of other events that did not look reassuring. It was only three decades later that Habib Ben Yahia, at the time the foreign minister, called for "the reconciliation of the sons of Abraham," and invited the Jews who had left Tunisia "to resume their ancient links with the open, tolerant country of theirs"—meaning Tunisia.[7]

Some Jews remained through all of the country's ups and downs, but at the time of Ben Ali's takeover, the Jewish community numbered only between 2,000 and 3,000. "We have never had any problems here as Jews, but the economic situation in the 1960s forced a gradual exodus," said Joseph Bismuth, owner of an automobile spare parts plant and a prominent member of Tunisia's Jewish community.[8]

Indeed, in the 1960s Tunisia's economic indicators were pointing downward, and, like most leaders of developing countries at the time, Bourguiba and his advisers opted for "socialism." And, step by step, the government was taking over the weak economic structure, an act discouraging to local businessmen as well as potential foreign investors.

The major event in 1962 was the departure of the large Algerian military force from western Tunisia and of the impressive political and propaganda apparatus from the capital itself. After seven years of guerrilla and terror war and the loss of an estimated million lives, Algeria became independent on July 3, 1962. The National Liberation Army (ALN), the revolution's military arm, held a last major parade on Tunisian soil in April, brandishing the heavy artillery and Chinese mortars it had been unable to infiltrate through the Morice Line. Thousands of Algerian refugees camping in western Tunisia applauded the show of strength which, unfortunately, was soon to be used in the bloody post-independence struggle for power. Throughout Algeria's turmoil of that summer, the Tunisians remained discreetly silent. Most were relieved that the Algerians had gone.

April brought a major event in Bourguiba's life: he married a woman described officially as his "childhood sweetheart," a member of a rich merchant family, Wassila Ben Amar. (Bourguiba had divorced his French wife who was the companion of his early political struggle and exile.) The wedding was a modest ceremony in La Marsa palace near the seashore, attended by members of the government and a handful of invited guests, including several reporters. Bourguiba had tears in his eyes and his plump bride, visibly uncomfortable in a tight and glittering wedding dress, sniffled gently. It made good copy.

Although ably assisted by several experienced diplomats in his foreign policy, Bourguiba chose for his chief economic reformer Ahmed Ben Salah, a young and ambitious technocrat who launched a costly and unproductive experiment in collective farms, nationalization of the medical profession, and other seemingly tempting facets of socialism. In 1964, Tunisia nationalized all French-owned farms without compensation, claiming that the land had been taken from Tunisians at the time of the protectorate. Immediately, France halted its economic aid and abolished preferential treatment for Tunisian products. Almost at the same time, the government ordered the closing of most Roman Catholic churches, feeling that the diminishing congregations did not warrant such a large number (about 70 throughout the country). The cathedrals in Carthage as well as in the heart of Tunis remained open, just as did the Great Synagogue on one of the capital's main thoroughfares, Rue de la Liberté. In the context of the post-colonial era, such decisions made sense but did not help Tunisia's reputation among Western countries.

While experimenting with socialism to find a solution for its permanent economic difficulties, Tunisia maintained a steady pro-Western course, including exceptionally good relations with the United States. During the first ten years of Tunisia's independence, Washington backed Bourguiba to the tune of half a billion dollars. To a great extent, Tunisia was a "test-tube of the effectiveness of American aid, a pro-American stronghold in an erratic Arab world, a rare country in Africa whose government gives total backing to the U.S. policy in Vietnam."[9] At that time communist bloc embassies in Tunis felt that Tunisia was unlikely to swerve from such a course because "it is too dependent on American money, too deeply committed." On the other hand, Western chanceries claimed that Tunisia "has never been radical," and that "the structure installed by Bourguiba is too solid to undergo drastic changes."[10] At 64, Bourguiba was still fiery, dynamic, magnetic, and captivating. One could see him walk briskly along the road between La Marsa and Carthage, followed by two or three body guards, always immaculate, with his trademark white scarf around his neck in the winter, waving at unprompted well-wishers.

Yet a quick look at the years between the Bizerta crisis and Bourguiba's serious heart attack early in 1967 shows a man vacillating between political options at home, trying nonalignment in foreign policy, hosting visiting communist dignitaries yet seriously limiting Tunisia's own left-wingers, lecturing fellow-Arabs on how to conduct their affairs and building around himself a cult of personality hardly in keeping with his international stature. Despite Tunisia's poverty which he ostensibly tried to combat, he had built for himself several ostentatious palaces equipped with such examples of doubtful taste as gold-plated doorknobs and transparent swimming pools. His speeches, broadcast on radio and television, still held crowds spellbound, and they ranged from cooking instructions for housewives to criticism of Egypt's Gamal Abdel Nasser.

In December 1962, Bourguiba intensified the fight against the followers of his late enemy Salah Ben Youssef, after the discovery of a mysterious "plot" apparently intended to depose him. The following year he banned the insignificant Tunisian Communist Party—and yet he hosted traveling

Chinese Prime Minister Chou En-lai. But throughout those years Bourguiba never changed his friendly feelings toward the United States, winning over successive U.S. ambassadors who justified his one-man, one-party rule as a necessary step in forging a nation after years of French colonial rule. In October 1963, Bourguiba ordered the ruling party's name changed from Neo-Destour to Socialist Destour Party (*Parti Socialiste Destourien*). The party allowed a certain degree of criticism of the functioning of the administrative apparatus, and some of its members were quite outspoken on occasion. One of the party's principles was a policy of "permanent dialogue between the summit and the grass-roots," a concept that has survived Bourguiba's political demise.

The party's influence was bolstered by the creation of the "Council of the Republic," an "inner sanctum" consisting of all cabinet ministers and members of the Destour Political Bureau. This body was a smoothly functioning group, and while some friction existed between its various members, there was no visible challenge to Bourguiba. The standard answer was *Na'am, Sidi Rais* (yes, Mr. President) and U.S. diplomatic dispatches often spoke of "benevolent dictatorship." Washington, it seems, accepted "Bourguibism" as Tunisia's line of conduct—with its "socialism, slogans, oversensitivity to criticism, diplomatic errors and the stubborn hope for a better future."[11]

His fellow Arabs were not so kind to Bourguiba, particularly when he tried to tell them how to run their affairs. In March 1965, Bourguiba embarked on a tour of the Middle East, including Egypt, Jordan, and Lebanon. Started amidst general indifference, the trip ended in a storm when Bourguiba delivered a lecture about his kind of "realpolitik." In short, he "advised" Middle Eastern Arabs to start negotiating with Israel and, in effect, accept the Jewish state in their midst. In a speech in Jericho, one of the more striking examples of Palestinian misery, he actually blamed the fate of the Palestinians on "the leaders of most states who do not face their responsibilities." The Arabs, concluded the indomitable Bourguiba in Jerusalem, "should proceed by stages—like Tunisia."

Those were fighting words, particularly at the time when Nasser was at the height of his power and unchallenged in the Arab political arena. "Who is this little man from North Africa trying to tell us what to do?," Arab diplomats sneered. In retrospect, the Tunisian "Supreme Warrior" was perfectly right and subsequent developments have vindicated him totally. But at the time his words were interpreted as a challenge to Nasser who felt that he alone was to decide what to do about Palestine and, indeed, all of the Middle East.

At home, on much more secure ground, Bourguiba was building his form of "socialism," a set of reforms reluctantly backed by Washington. Bourguiba's pro-U.S. policies, Tunisia's compactness, the cohesion of the people, and the strength of the ruling party seemed to U.S. diplomats a reasonable guarantee of success, regardless of the socialist label. Despite a bad drought in 1966 which cut the growth of the Gross National Product from 5 percent to 2 percent, Tunisia was developing. Factories, schools, and public buildings were being built throughout the country. A major achievement was the hotel industry, attracting increasing numbers of Europeans to Tunisia's almost perfect sandy beaches. Tourist revenue eventually became the main foreign currency earner, but in the mid-1960s Tunisia struggled with its cash flow. There were occasions when funds had to be scraped from several banks to provide departing Tunisian delegations with necessary money for travel.

The period that followed was often referred to by Tunisians alarmed at the country's slide as "the years of uncertainty." Indeed, while it was obvious that Bourguiba was desperately searching for friends and for solutions, his actions seemed spasmodic. In 1967, he stopped boycotting the Arab League, offered support (verbal) to Nasser after the disastrous war with Israel, and allowed a mob to stage a noisy demonstration outside the U.S. embassy in Tunis. The damage was minor, but Washington began to wonder about the solidity of U.S.-Tunisian friendship. There were no spontaneous demonstrations in Tunisia in those days, and American diplomats blamed the government-controlled Tunis radio for inciting the masses. Virtually on the heels of the riot, Bourguiba dispatched Bahi Ladgham, his number 2 man, to inspect the damaged building and offer the government's apologies.

In 1968, a series of trials involving various, rather insignificant, left-wing activists were held amidst rumors of conspiracy. Bourguiba's wrath then shifted to his economy minister, Ahmed Ben Salah, author of socialist experiments, among which some 350,000 hectares (close to 900,000 acres) of land previously held by French "colons" were turned into cooperatives. There was a lot of talk about the modernization of agriculture and its integration into the national economy. According to the progressive French-language monthly *Le Nouvel Afrique Asie*, the reforms failed "because of the excess of heavy-handed and paralyzing bureaucracy, which left no room for maneuver for peasants it claimed to modernize."[12] Ben Salah was fired and subsequently jailed. He managed to escape to Algeria and later to Libya, where he founded, in 1973, the "Popular Unity Movement," an organization that never presented any significant challenge to Bourguiba and his system of governance.

Then, in 1974, Bourguiba astounded the world by announcing a "union" with Libya, its southern neighbor, whose president, Moammer Gadhafi, had begun to preach his "green revolution." Even the most enthusiastic Tunisian admirers of Bourguiba began to doubt his judgment, indeed, even his mental capacity to govern. "For me, he (Bourguiba) died in January, 1974, in Djerba, when during several minutes of face-to-face with Gadhafi, he signed, on hotel stationery, that famous charter of union," wrote Tunisian journalist Bechir Ben Yahmed.[13] It was the time when courtiers quoted Bourguiba's wife as saying that he was "like a candelabrum of 100 candles of which 70 are extinguished." A Swiss psychologist was said to have warned Bourguiba's advisers shortly afterward that "from now on, you will have many such 'Djerbas.' You ought to be very careful."[14]

But the old president was sacrosanct, and no one was prepared to mention the question of his succession. Predictably, the "union treaty" was quickly forgotten, thrown into the dustbin of history. A year later, Bourguiba demanded a constitutional amendment to allow him to become president-for-life. Relations with Libya worsened, and during 1976 thousands of Tunisian workers were expelled by Gadhafi. Four years later, the southern oasis of Gafsa was the scene of bloody clashes, fomented by Libya which dispatched a commando of saboteurs to blow up a pipeline and spread chaos.

Labor unrest was steadily growing in Tunisia, leading to a strike in 1978 called by the General Union of Tunisian Workers (UGTT). Clashes with security forces ended in a bloodbath, with dozens killed. The government clamped a state of emergency on the country. A new wave of incidents erupted in 1984, when the government increased the price of bread. The incidents have since become known as "bread riots." Tunisia was no longer a docile country, but its president remained unperturbed. He was surrounded by sycophants or men incapable of telling him the truth.

The picture of Tunisia in the twilight of the power of the "grand monsieur" was not a happy one. The labor unions had been broken and existed in name only; the opposition press had been muzzled. No one had dared to address the dramatic problem of the young generation which was being educated but not employed. Underneath the facade of an obedient and cheerful press lay a web of palace intrigue, frantic maneuvers by courtiers trying to manipulate the old man, arrests, charges of corruption and even seizures of seagoing yachts to make sure their owners did not leave the country. Western chanceries in Tunis were in a state of confusion. Several countries had invested considerable sums of money in Tunisia's future, banking on the survival of a form of "Bourguibism" with its moderate influence in the Arab world and, despite the dogmatic leader, a relatively open society. By 1986, the United States had pumped in about $1.5 billion in aid to Tunisia, putting the country among the leading per capita recipients of American largesse.

Meanwhile, the educational system, one of the main achievements of "Bourguibism," had begun to crumble. Only 13 percent of the country's secondary-school pupils passed examinations in 1986 because they were taken in Arabic rather than in French, amidst general unrest in educational institutions and an acerbic debate about advantages and disadvantages of "Arabization." Bourguiba seemed distant from the problem. That year, with one stroke of his pen, he divorced his second wife, claiming she "contradicted him." A new "éminence grise" emerged into the limelight in the seaside Carthage palace, Madame Saida Sassi, a strong-willed woman with a coterie of her own, who soon dominated the old president.

From the economic point of view, the situation was worsening. In August 1986, Bourguiba summoned his rubber-stamp parliament for an emergency session and instructed the recently named prime minister, Rachid Sfar, to bluntly spell out the facts and the planned austerity measures. They included more budgetary restrictions, cuts in imports, and general belt-tightening moves. Diplomats described the measures as involving "a high degree of risk."[15]

The crisis was played out against a backdrop of summer vacation stupor, crowded seaside cafes, and jasmine-scented evenings. To an unsuspecting visitor, the coastal suburbs of Tunis offered a picture-postcard vista of blue sea and sky, dazzlingly white villas sheltered by Mediterranean greenery. Tunisians, sipping mint tea, bitterly described the country's economy as a "sinking ship" or an airplane whose pilot is desperately trying all controls, none of which respond.[16]

All main sources of revenue had been falling for some time: oil, remittances from Tunisian workers abroad, income from phosphate exports, and even income from tourism despite attractive prices. Mohammed Mzali, who was dismissed as premier in July, had failed to come up with any realistic solutions. After praising Mzali as "my successor and my son in whom I have absolute confidence," at the congress of the Destour Party in June, Bourguiba then proceeded to replace him with Sfar, a 52-year-old economist. Mzali tried to leave the country in August on a Geneva-bound plane but was prevented by police. Later, he managed to cross into Algeria and, from there, to Switzerland, where he received asylum on the condition that he refrained from making political statements. He arranged to meet journalists in an elegant hotel in the nearby French spa of Divonne. There he stated he did not blame Bourguiba for anything because the president was manipulated by courtiers "for the sake of power." He said he hoped that Bourguiba would "find a moment of lucidity" and remove the advisers who "were pushing the country toward political extremism." He particularly singled out Madame Sassi who engineered Bourguiba's divorce and even his estrangement from his son, Habib Bourguiba, Jr.[17]

To calm the restive schools and universities, Bourguiba ordered examinations for the "baccalauréat" (diploma at the end of secondary education) to be taken again, in September—and in French. Presumably, in "a moment of lucidity," the president decided that Mzali's "Arabization program" did not turn Tunisians into brilliant Arabists but merely reduced their knowledge of French.

But by then, unrest among the young was hard to contain. Demonstrations and strikes multiplied at the three universities existing at that time, causing repeated police incursions into the campuses and seriously damaging what was to be the last academic year under Bourguiba's rule.

In Tunisia, the problem of the young was crucial. During Bourguiba's last year in power, 60 percent of Tunisia's population was under the age of 25, and 50 percent under 20. Most of the unemployed were among the young, whose standard complaint was that "the state has given us education but no jobs." It is difficult to discern to what extent Bourguiba, once a grand old man with a vision, understood the question and its impact.

The economic woes, the unsolved problems, and the growing frustration of the young turned out to be an unusual opportunity for a new movement sweeping the Arab world—that of Islamic fundamentalism. Officially peaceful and claiming only to want "true democracy" in a religious spirit, the movement had far-reaching political ambitions which in other countries caused major economic setbacks if not disasters. During Bourguiba's last years in his Carthage palace, fundamentalism represented a major threat to the country that he wanted secular and Westernized.

NOTES

1. Habib Bourguiba in conversation with the author.
2. Hedi Mechri of *L'Économiste Maghrebin* in conversation with the author.
3. Author's dispatch in the French daily *Le Monde*, April 1960.
4. Author's dispatch in *The Washington Post*, 25 April 1960.
5. Youssef Kadouk in conversation with the author.
6. Habib Bourguiba in conversation with the author.
7. Habib Ben Yahia in conversation with the author.
8. Joseph Bismuth in conversation with the author.
9. Author's dispatch in *The Washington Star*, 11 April 1967.
10. Author's notes.
11. U.S. Embassy's cable to Washington, D.C., April 1967.
12. *Le Nouvel Afrique Asie*, June 1996.
13. Bechir Ben Yahmed, *Jeune Afrique*, 18 November 1987.
14. Ibid.
15. Author's interviews.
16. Ibid.
17. Mohammed Mzali in conversation with the author.

CHAPTER 4

Fired by Islam

On August 2, 1987, bombs exploded at four hotels in Monastir, Habib Bourguiba's birthplace: Hana Beach, Hannibal Palace, Le Kuriat, and Sahara Beach, marring the celebrations of the Tunisian president's birthday. It was also the height of the tourist season, and, to the outside world, the explosions signaled a warning that Tunisia was no longer a safe haven from the turmoil then affecting much of the Arab world.

The scenario, as outlined later by Tunisian officials and historians, could have been disastrous: more strikes at universities, street demonstrations directed from radicalized mosques, and a putsch set for November 8, exploiting the deteriorating economic situation and a growing dissatisfaction in the face of a lack of firm and enlightened leadership. Following the nomination of Zine Al Abidine Ben Ali as interior minister and then prime minister, the events took another, salutary, turn, sparing Tunisia the fate of Iran, Sudan, and Afghanistan—or the savage terror of Algeria. On November 7 of that year, Ben Ali deposed the weakening "president-for-life" and launched a program he likes to describe as that of "national reconciliation." Although some chroniclers, diplomats, and historians disagree about the extent of the danger facing Tunisia in those days, it is now reasonably clear that Ben Ali's move came at a critical time, saving the country from an uncertain fate, heavy in internal and international consequences.

By the time the bombs planted by Islamic militants shattered Tunisia's precarious peace, the term "Islamic fundamentalism" had become a major issue in the West. To some Islamists, the West had replaced the fear of communism with that of a rising Islamic power which rejected the Western way of life and its form of democracy. Bourguiba himself joined the ranks of those who considered Islamic fundamentalism to be a new global threat.

The scope of the Islamic resurgence "has been worldwide, embracing much of the Muslim world from the Sudan to Indonesia. Heads of Muslim governments as well as opposition groups increasingly appealed to religion for legitimacy and to mobilize popular support."[1] In Tunisia's progressive circles, the rise of political Islam was seen as a major threat to everything that the country had previously stood for.

The characteristics of the looming confrontation had been watched with concern—even alarm—since the early 1980s, when Islamists had begun their policy of infiltrating various state institutions, including universities, religious schools, the police, and the army. While the earlier Tunisian Islamist movement had been a marginal force, in the 1980s "it made spectacular gains, becoming the second largest political force in the country."[2]

Historians of modern-age Tunisia trace the roots of the Islamist struggle to several factors. Among them were the decay of social and economic conditions, and the temptation of religion as a solution to the apparent failure of the Western democratic system. In the early period, the movement was known as *al-Jama'a al-Islamiyya*, and its objectives were mainly to revive religious feelings in society. Thus it concentrated its activities on mosques, schools, and charitable institutions. "It was characterized by social conservatism and by intellectual political limitations. It promoted its views through publications such as *al-Ma'rifa*, *al-Mujtama* and *al-Habib*, virtually taking them over."[3]

As time went by, the concept of Islam as a political weapon penetrated the labor unions, the press, and academic circles, becoming a sort of escape valve in the atmosphere of a growing paralysis at the top of the Tunisian power pyramid.

In the early 1980s, when Bourguiba announced his intention of introducing political pluralism, the Islamists surged to the fore, creating the "Islamic Tendency Movement" (MTI—Mouvement de la Tendance Islamique). The MTI multiplied press conferences and statements and quickly gained support among intellectual circles for which it was an alternative to the dominant Destour Party. It was a period that saw the emergence of a new type of Islamic leadership "that included professionals, manipulators of the masses, communications specialists, masters in swaying public opinion and experts in logistics. This generation of organizers, engineers and professionals was seizing the leadership from the established orators and cultural exponents."[4]

It was during that period that the Tunisian Islamists began to draft a plan not just to increase their influence in the country but to seize power—by any means available, including violence.

June 6, 1981, was a significant date in the history of the Tunisian Islamic movement: the election of Rachid Ghannouchi as president of the MTI. The

40-year-old Ghannouchi came from a humble background. He was one of the ten children of a poor farming family in the southern province of Gabès. After the usual Franco-Arabic primary education, he moved to the Koranic schools, and then to the "Zitouna system," named after the famous mosque in Tunis and the leading center of the country's Islamic learning. Subsequently he studied in Cairo and Damascus and dabbled in journalism in arch-communist Albania. In 1968 he went to Paris, where he considerably improved his knowledge of French, neglected during his Koranic studies. On returning to Tunis in 1969, he taught philosophy in secondary school and became active in the nascent Islamic movement.

Ghannouchi styled himself a rising star on the Islamic horizon and that is why the above brief sketch of his life is important. His statements and writings show a striking evolution from moderation to extremism. Some Tunisians believe that he always believed in extreme solutions to introduce political Islam. However, his departure from Tunisia in 1989 removed him from the mainstream of Islamic thought and activity and reduced him to strident attacks on Tunisia, its leadership and system from the safe distance of his exile.

Suspected of contacts with Iran during the period preceding his election to the MTI's presidency, Ghannouchi was arrested and sentenced to 11 years in prison. He was released three years later in a presidential amnesty. But "his imprisonment added to the sense of martyrdom, and with his conviction in 1987 he was sentenced to life imprisonment at hard labor. Bourguiba's desire to change the sentence to death helped provoke Ben Ali's overthrow of Bourguiba."[5]

Following his release from prison, Ghannouchi chose the road of exile and made statements from Algiers, Paris, and London, apparently traveling on a Sudanese passport. He also spent some time in Iran. Gradually, he became friendly with other well-known and controversial Islamic leaders, including Abassi Madani, head of Algeria's Islamic Salvation Front (FIS), and Hassan al-Turabi, the chief ideologue of Sudan's military regime.

The initial objectives of the MTI seemed benign and concentrated on religious and philosophical issues. Thus the movement called for efforts to "revive the Islamic personality of Tunisia," renew Islamic thought, "purify it of the effects of centuries of decadence," and "contribute to the re-birth of the political and civilizational entity of Islam. . . . To save our peoples and all humanity from psychic error, social injustice, and international hegemony."

Ghannouchi was a popular orator and preacher, and his appearances almost always drew crowds. He was a man with a self-styled mission to restore Tunisia to its Arab-Islamic roots, and, according to all indications, he believed in his cause.

To attain its objectives, the MTI proposed a tame program including the increasing importance of the mosque as a cultural magnet, intense lectures and debate of Islamic concepts and values, and the consolidation of Arabization in education. Mentioned in the program, as if in passing, were also such aims as the consolidation of trade union activities, the "liberation of Islamic consciousness from cultural and civilization submission," and, perhaps the most telling objective, the "effective support for national liberation movements in the world." Much stronger rhetoric, calling for the abolition of established order, came later, confirming the Tunisian government's charges of conspiracy to seize power. Two years after his self-imposed exile, Ghannouchi admitted that during its evolution, the Islamic movement intended to "impose popular change," whatever that meant. And, he added,

As far as we are concerned, we do not deny this part of the plot. After 10 years of fruitless attempts to act in accord with the law, we have considered that pursuing this way would be to mislead the people and chase after mirages. Therefore, we have decided to impose change by the people.[6]

The Tunisian government felt all along that the MTI had adopted "Sudanese tactics" of takeover, consisting of infiltration of the apparatus of the state and its institutions, followed by "Islamization of the street." Mosques with their loudspeakers seemed an easy way to propagate the MTI's political message. Equally easy were educational institutions, already in a state of unrest. The demise of Mzali as prime minister in July 1986, accompanied by yet another change in political and economic guidelines, was seen by the Islamists as a good opportunity to advance their cause.

Previously, the Islamists had benefited from the 1984 "bread riots," and during the Mzali premiership there were definite signs that he considerably facilitated Islamic inroads in the country—and even courted the movement. Like the MTI, Mzali favored Arabization of the educational system, feeling that under the prevailing program "our young speak neither good French nor adequate Arabic."[7] It was clear that Mzali's removal represented a major loss for the Islamists.

The key of the MTI plan was the "ripening of the fruit," a concept that consisted of persuading "the street" that solutions could no longer come from the regime in power but from Islamists seeking to seize it. In preparation for the coup planned at the latest for Sunday, November 8, 1987, the Islamists obtained a *fatwa* (a decree by a Muslim jurist on a specific subject) exonerating them from guilt for killing other Muslims.[8]

Thus prepared, the Islamists multiplied street demonstrations, meetings, and large-scale political agitation. State prisons were so infiltrated by Islamic activists that jailed leaders had no difficulty in transmitting orders to the outside. Prison walls were simply "porous."[9] At the same time, in addition to the mainstream movement, there was a proliferation of other groups, often small and more virulent in criticizing the government, with programs varying from communism to pan-Arabism. This further confused the political scene.

For Bourguiba, the rise of the Islamic movement represented a threat to all the values he had introduced in Tunisia, mainly a Western-type secular society. The old president may have been weak and easily maneuvered in the latter years of his rule, but he remained vigilant when it came to religious inroads in politics. To him, the Islamists represented "the vestiges of an outdated religious traditionalism"[10] and an assault on his achievements. His fury was such that when the courts sentenced Ghannouchi to life imprisonment after his arrest in March 1987, Bourguiba demanded a new trial. He wanted Ghannouchi dead.

Despite considerable success by the authorities in the fight against the Islamic groups and their sympathizers in the second half of 1987, the Islamic problem continued to haunt the Tunisian leadership. In October of that year, Bourguiba named Ben Ali, then interior minister, to the post of prime minister. A man with extensive security training, Ben Ali helped re-establish the confidence of the business community in Tunisia's future by taking energetic steps against the Islamists as well as by issuing a number of decrees aimed at reviving the moribund economy. The security measures included the infiltration of university campuses, intensified surveillance of mosques as well as of airports and other points of entry. The Tunisian government firmly believed that the Islamist movement was subsidized from abroad, mainly from Iran. When the Iranian embassy in Tunis was shut down by the authorities, a jubilant Tunisian official said, "drifters can no longer count on five dinars (then about $6) for setting cars on fire."[11]

After conferring with representatives of the main Tunisian civil rights groups, the new prime minister assured Western diplomats that his strong-arm methods were temporary and were made necessary by Tunisia's infiltration by revolutionary elements. In a conversation with then U.S. Ambassador Robert H. Pelletreau, Ben Ali described the task ahead of him as "consolidating the republican system, strengthening its institutions, confirming the rule of law and safeguarding national achievements."[12]

It was significant that on November 13, less than a week after Ben Ali's takeover of the presidency, Abdelfattah Mourou, one of the leaders of the MTI who was in exile in Saudi Arabia, praised the overthrow of Bourguiba. According to one assessment of the takeover, "the events of 7 November, which ushered in a new era for Tunisia and for the Maghreb, benefited two main groups: the followers of Ben Ali and the Islamists. The relationship between the new leaders and the MTI was characterized by realism, a certain degree of affinity, and also some controversy."[13]

With the skill he was to demonstrate subsequently on a number of occasions, Ben Ali launched a new policy toward Islamists. Although full of nuance, it was intended, by conciliatory measures, to reduce the appeal of militant Islam, replacing it with a moderate, and thus controllable, version. Consequently, Islam was reaffirmed as the national religion, and gestures were made toward what the authorities considered to be moderate Islamic groups, while, at the same time, strict laws were drafted on the punishment for subversive acts committed in the name of Islam.

Echoing the statement by Mourou, the exiled MTI leader, the local Islamic leadership rushed to promise cooperation with the new president. The Islamists described the takeover as an historic event and "a divine act to save the country from a civil war created and maintained by the former president." In a letter to Ben Ali, the MTI leadership said it wanted to "leave the past behind, engage in dialogue without reservations or preoccupations, support the stability and security of the country, and contribute to achieving everything that (your) appeal of 7 November entails."[14]

The government responded, during the following months, with more concessions to the Islamists, thus ushering in a period of relative optimism vis-à-vis Tunisia's major problem. The concessions included an amnesty for MTI prisoners, the right for the MTI to be represented in the High Islamic Council created by the government, participation by Islamists in drafting a program of cooperation among all political tendencies (known as the National Pact) as well as authorization for the Islamists to take part in general elections.

But polite exchanges with the MTI and gestures toward its members did not satisfy the extremist Islamic elements. Before the end of November, 191 persons, including 57 military personnel, were arrested on charges of fomenting a plot that included plans to assassinate leading government officials and widespread attacks on civilian and military targets, including the presidential palace, radio and television stations, and the defense and interior ministries. The MTI itself was not implicated—or even mentioned when the plot of the so-called "Security Group" was officially announced.

During the subsequent two years, following intense negotiations between government officials and several Islamic leaders, all those arrested were released. The reasons for such a magnanimous gesture were never fully explained. Surely, if the detainees were guilty of the serious crimes against the state of which they were initially accused, some sort of punishment must have been required? But, apparently, the government intended to try all sorts of "carrot" approaches to defuse the potentially explosive situation.

New decisions and announcements followed swiftly after the takeover. The Call to Prayer was broadcast again on radio and television, thus removing its suspension by Bourguiba who was obsessed by secularism. New institutions were established to protect mosques, and the faculty of theology at the university in Tunis was allowed to use its old name banned by Bourguiba—Zitouna. Finally, about 2,500 persons held in jail or under house arrest for Islamic activities were released. Other releases were to follow as Ben Ali accentuated his policy of national reconciliation. Thus, in

May 1988, Ghannouchi was freed from prison, and by the end of the year most, if not all, MTI leaders were free or returning from exile. Although all signs pointed to a new era in the relationship between the government and Islamists, future events were to perturb such a promising beginning for the Change.

Nonetheless, the Islamists remained watchful and mistrustful, sensing their appeal to be threatened by Ben Ali's measures. They were particularly alarmed by a new law regarding political parties, adopted May 12, 1988, which banned groups with programs based on "religion, language, race or region." The wording of the law was carefully crafted, but its main objective was to prevent the spread of "political Islam" which Bourguiba had fought in a blunt and crude fashion but which Ben Ali intended to return to its original place, that is the mosque, while keeping in mind the strong religious feelings of his overwhelmingly Muslim constituency.

Marring the improving relationship between church and state was "the Bardo incident," during which a pregnant lawyer, Radhia Nasraoui, was physically attacked by slogan-shouting demonstrators at a human rights meeting in a Tunis suburb known for its world-famous museum of Roman mosaics. There was little doubt that Islamists were to blame, and the Tunisian media did not spare criticism.

As the general elections scheduled for April 2, 1989, approached, it was clear that the government would not—and according to the law could not—tolerate a party openly flaunting its Islamic message, that is the MTI. Less than two months before the vote, the MTI requested recognition as *al-Nahda* (the name of *Ennahda* was also used), or renaissance in Arabic. In a crude fashion, the Islamists thus wanted to circumvent the law on political parties as well as the National Pact in which they had agreed to cooperate with Ben Ali's guidelines. The Tunisians authorities were aware that while using that camouflage for electoral purposes, the MTI was also busy constructing a parallel underground structure with clearly revolutionary aims.

In the end, the Islamists decided to present their candidates as "independents," vying for 129 seats out of the 141 at stake. "The government's attitude seems to have been somewhat ambivalent. It continued to resist formally al-Nahda as a political party, insisting that no party could claim a monopoly on religion. . . . Yet it also permitted the party to run candidates and campaign openly."[15] Once again, Ben Ali and his government showed they intended to avoid any confrontation with the movement that could harm the country's peaceful evolution.

Under the French-style proportional electoral system adopted by Tunisia, major political groups were favored and, consequently, the Constitutional Democratic Rally (the reformed Destour Socialist Party) won 80 percent of the vote and all seats at stake. Nonetheless, Islamist candidates obtained 14.6 percent of the vote, but, in areas such as Tunis with its large and impoverished suburbs, 30 percent. As far as the government was concerned, the message was clear: the Islamists had not been defeated and still had considerable appeal in "the street." The Islamists read the results of the vote as encouraging further action. A little over one year later, amidst a tense precombat vigil, Ghannouchi left the country. He was thus absent when, in the following years, the state and armed religion clashed openly, and Tunisia's fate hung in the balance.

A decision by the Islamic movement to revert to plans of armed action to facilitate a takeover was caused, according to all indications, by its failure to achieve success at the polls. Although the Islamists could count on a considerable following among the poor of the capital, the national figure fell below their initial expectations. Although a signal of alarm to the government, the 14.6 percent was significantly lower than that, for example, of the Islamist Refah (Welfare) Party in Turkey in 1995. With a little over 22 percent of the vote, Refah could—and did—aspire to the status of a major political force and its leader, Necmettin Erbakan, to premiership. The Tunisian Islamists could nurture no such hopes through the normal democratic process, and Western diplomats, urging a democratic solution with Islamic participation, were considered by many in Tunisia to be hopelessly naive. A statement "what the West does not understand is that those who claim moderation only appear to be moderate and that there is a dagger underneath every djellaba," summarizes the feelings of many educated Tunisians.[16]

While preparing for a major armed confrontation, al-Nahda faced a serious internal crisis caused by the Iraqi invasion of Kuwait in August 1990. The Tunisian government condemned the invasion but opposed the use of force by the international coalition (see subsequent chapters). Al-Nahda favored Iraq, but its funds came to a large extent from Saudi Arabia which was the staging area for the 1991 Operation Desert Storm.

The crisis and subsequent war helped exacerbate already existing splits within the movement. It brought these splits into the open, though in fact no elements within al-Nahda were openly sympathetic with the Western intervention. It was widely believed, however, that there were many who supported Saudi Arabia and Kuwait.[17]

Faced with reports of the formation of new armed cells in which members of al-Nahda were involved, the government returned to the policy of vigilance and prevention. In December 1990, over 100 supporters of al-Nahda were jailed, and the Islamist newspaper *al-Fajr* was shut down. These events generally escaped the attention of the international media, preoccupied with the military buildup for attack on the Iraqi forces in Kuwait.

As events unfolded in the Gulf area in February 1991, Tunisia was confronted with a new phenomenon: a brutal attack on the office of the ruling Constitutional Democratic Rally in the Tunis suburb of Bab Souika. During the attack by a special al-Nahda commando, two guards of the building were seized, tied up, doused with gasoline, and torched. One died, the other had to undergo amputation and remained in a coma for months. Those accused of the attack were apprehended, judged, and five among them were sentenced to death (two of them in absentia).

In many ways, the Islamists played into the government's hands. They bared their teeth in a manner to which the Tunisian public was not accustomed in a country known for its tradition of nonviolence. Although there were other attacks on government and party officials during which men were blinded and disfigured by vitriol, the Bab Souika incident was a milestone in the confrontation between the Tunisian state and the Islamists. Eventually, it also caused a sharp drop in support for the Islamic movement.

According to Abdelbaki Hermassi, minister of culture in 1997,

the Bab Souika attack was the turning point. The Islamists showed they could not succeed in the electoral process and had adopted a policy of violence. All the regime had to do was to draw conclusions—and it did. It was a major mistake by the Islamists and the regime exploited it intelligently.[18]

Thus, the violent turn of events weakened al-Nahda and increased its internal rifts. Abdelfattah Mourou, one of the movement's "historic leaders," announced he had "frozen" his membership in the organization and accused Ghannouchi, who was in exile, of opting for a policy of violence. Mourou himself said he favored dialogue.

Al-Nahda of the early 1990s days had a highly developed structure, devised mainly during a clandestine "congress" in the southern city of Sfax. Its head, known as emir, was Sadok Chourou, a pharmacist by education and subsequently a university lecturer. It had an executive bureau, which supervised such key departments as those of organization and administration, information, education, labor unions, and of "cultural and social mobilization."

The official structure had a parallel secret organization whose job was to plot the overthrow of the regime, and thus turn Tunisia into an Islamic state. Known as the "Special Apparatus," this organization had a structure similar to most subversive movements around the world, including intelligence, security, and training departments. It paid particular attention to the recruitment of military personnel and to contacts in the customs and border police in order to facilitate the smuggling of weapons and the infiltration of agents from abroad. Its plan of action was relatively simple and consisted of a preparatory phase, characterized by slogan-painting and the distribution of tracts, which was to be gradually escalated to marches and street demonstrations. Further phases envisaged attacks on government, military, and party officials which would be accompanied by unrest in schools and universities. One of the objectives was to provoke the security forces to open fire on unarmed civilians, thus discrediting the regime. The final stage was to consist of getting the army involved in maintaining law and order—and to subjugate it through a network of previously created Islamic cells. The government would then fall into the Islamist lap—"like a ripe fruit."[19]

Further proof of al-Nahda's plans to escalate the conflict was a letter from Ghannouchi in which he apparently wrote, "we consider it a good omen that the number of victims is growing. We want martyrs." On May 22, 1991, Interior Minister Abdallah Kallel said the authorities had thwarted a plan to seize the key government ministries and the major centers of communications. A year later, he said, "nothing was ignored by the conspirators, including my own assassination."[20]

The key actors in the takeover operation, code-named Divine Mission, had been trained in three camps outside the Sudanese capital Khartoum, according to Kallel. Iran provided most of the funds and instructors. "Our friends in the West do not realize the seriousness of the problem," Kallel said. "The fundamentalists still believe in jihad (holy war) against Christianity and in the return to the sources of Islam. We are all Muslims here but we also want to be part of the civilized community of nations, not prisoners of fanatical clerics."

According to documents seized by the authorities at the time, the expansion of the Islamic underground movement followed a five-point plan which was to culminate in commando operations by teams of 19 men in each of the country's *gouvernorats* (administrative regions). The military action was to be preceded by intense infiltration of the school system. According to French security estimates, at one stage Islamists controlled 109 out of Tunisia's 588 secondary schools.

Because an attack on the heavily fortified and guarded presidential palace was considered doomed in advance, the plotters planned to obtain a U.S. Stinger missile from Afghanistan to shoot down Ben Ali's plane as it was taking off for one of his periodic trips abroad, Kallel said. The statement caused controversy, because U.S. officials claimed no such missile could have arrived in Tunisia in time for the planned action on October 15, 1991. However, Washington acknowledged that some Stingers sent to the Afghan *mujaheddin* fighting the Soviet forces may have found their way to other countries, including Algeria. The al-Nahda plotters apparently hoped to obtain such a weapon from Algerian fundamentalists.

Algeria, with its well-developed Islamic network, was indeed the main external base of the Tunisian fundamentalists. In fact, both Tunisian Islamists and the government watched the events in its large neighbor to the west, each for a different reason. The Islamists feared that they might lose a convenient base in the event of a major clampdown on the Algerian militants, while the government feared a fallout of Algeria's vicissitudes. Thus Tunisian Islamists triumphed when Algeria recognized the Islamic Salvation Front (FIS) while the Tunisian government worried about possible repercussions. The dramatic gains by FIS in the first round of legislative elections in December 1991, and the virtual certainty that it would win the second round, caused the cancellation of the vote by a worried government in Algiers. The Algerian Islamists went underground, and their extreme wing soon launched a major terror war which horrified the world. During the first five years of that bloody confrontation more than 60,000 people were slaughtered, including women and children.

The extent of the Algerian Islamic terror has totally vindicated Ben Ali and his government's policy toward that religious movement. In the first years following the Change, the regime tried almost everything to co-opt the Islamists and proved to be extremely generous with amnesties for culprits. It was only after such attacks as the one in Bab Souika that security measures were tightened and a more severe course was taken. The Tunisians no longer needed to cite Iran or Sudan as being examples of what happens to a country when the Islamists take over. Terror by groups next door that claimed to act in the name of God was far more outspoken. As one Tunisian said later, "the fundamentalists wanted to Algerianize us. Ben Ali saved the country twice, first when he saved it from Bourguiba and then from the Islamists."[21]

From his various external bases, Ghannouchi continued to comment on the events in Algeria, concluding that "the Algerian affair did us a great disservice and gave our adversaries the opportunity to appear threatened. It created the impression that the West needed them to face the danger that is spreading from Algeria toward Europe."[22]

By mid-1992, many Tunisians believed that their own Islamic problem was contained, although not completely stifled. Certainly, the universities were calm after several years of turbulence during which education was disrupted by political and religious agitation. As Education Minister Mohamed Charfi, who lectured at Tunis University during that difficult period, recalled,

I used to walk into the auditorium, start my lecture and usually after 10 minutes or so they [students] would sing prayers. I waited until they finished and resumed the lecture. There was more singing, usually by a small group sitting together, and slogan shouting. The rest of the class usually did not interfere. Eventually I had to leave, my continued presence there made no sense.

"And imagine" he added, "when the ringleaders were arrested, their families rushed to complain to the Tunisian Human Rights League. It was a painful choice: either arrest the instigators or allow chaos to grow and reign."[23]

While Ghannouchi continued thundering from abroad about the alleged persecution of the Islamists, historians began debating whether the radicalization of al-Nahda was the result of its leadership's long-standing tendency or that of reaction to government suppression measures. According to John L. Esposito,

Tunisia's Renaissance Party provides an example of the radicalization of movements in response to government manipulation of the political system, suppression, or violence. Increased government repression intimidates, factionalizes, and radicalizes. The result has been an escalation of confrontation and violence.[24]

This theory is firmly rejected by the Tunisian government, which points to myriad overtures to the Islamists by Ben Ali after his 1987 takeover. Had the Islamists honored their pledge of democratic cooperation and the National Pact, to which they subscribed, there would have been no need or reason for any government clampdown, Tunisian officials say.

Esposito further argues that "though the Renaissance Party avoided confrontational politics in the early years of Ben Ali's rule, the government's decision not to recognize it as a legal party and violation of human rights to intimidate its members, led the Renaissance Party to denounce the government for authoritarianism."[25] To prove his argument, he cites an article in *The Economist* of May 18, 1991, saying,

his [Ben Ali's] party, the Constitutional Democratic Rally, rigged the poll in the 1989 general election and took every seat in the parliament. Far from legalizing the leading opposition group, the president has sought to crush it. . . .There is no real democracy and no press freedom.

To the Tunisian government, the choice was between clamping down on Islamists or facing death by terror.

To Michael Collins Dunn, Ghannouchi's argument after the discovery of the 1991 plot was that "the state can never give the Islamists the rights they demand, and must therefore be overthrown."[26] Such a way of thinking, according to Dunn, "violates everything he (Ghannouchi) said or wrote for many years."

By 1996 the situation in Tunisia was such that government officials boldly announced that "the population has been vaccinated against fundamentalism."[27] But because neighboring Algeria was in the throes of Islamic violence, Tunisia remained in a state of permanent alert. There was no other solution. Once again, events in Algeria cast a long shadow over its eastern neighbor, as they did during the 1954–1962 war of independence.

NOTES

1. John L. Esposito, *The Islamic Threat: Myth or Reality?* (New York: Oxford University Press, 1992), p. 11.

2. Abdelbaki Hermassi, *The Islamist Dilemma* (Ithaca: Laura Guazzone, 1992), p. 105.

3. Ibid., p. 106.

4. Ibid., p. 108.

5. Michael C. Dunn, *Renaissance or Radicalism? Political Islam: The Case of Tunisia's al-Nahda* (Washington, D.C.: International Estimate, 1992), pp. 21–22.

6. Rachid Ghannouchi writing in *Arabies*, July–August, 1991.

7. Mohammed Mzali in conversation with the author.

8. Sadok Chaabane, *Ben Ali et la Voie Pluraliste en Tunisie* (Tunis: Ceres Editions, 1996), p. 46.

9. Ibid.

10. Esposito, *The Islamic Threat*, p. 160.

11. Author's dispatch in *The Washington Times*, 26 October, 1987.

12. Robert Pelletreau in conversation with the author.

13. Hermassi, *The Islamic Dilemma*, p. 109.

14. Tunisian government archives.

15. Dunn, *Renaissance or Radicalism?*, p. 47.

16. Chaabane, *Ben Ali et la Voie Pluraliste*, p. 43.

17. Dunn, *Renaissance or Radicalism?*, p. 53.

18. Abdelbaki Hermassi in conversation with the author.

19. Ibid.

20. Abdallah Kallel in conversation with the author.

21. Mustapha Khammari, Tunisian journalist, in conversation with the author.

22. Hermassi, *The Islamic Dilemma*, p. 125.

23. Author's dispatch in *The Washington Times*, 5 May 1992.

24. Esposito, *The Islamic Threat*, p. 163.

25. Ibid., p. 162.

26. Dunn, *Renaissance or Radicalism?*, p. 107.

27. Oussama Romdhani, senior Tunisian official, in conversation with the author.

CHAPTER 5

On With the New

While the threat of Islamic fundamentalism remained Tunisia's preoccupation until Bourguiba's last days in power and, indeed, throughout most of the first ten years of the Change, in the autumn of 1987 the overriding question was the president's increasingly apparent senility. The Carthage palace was a hive of plots and counterplots, of schemes to manipulate the aging statesman, and of plans on how to reduce the influence of some members of the government or to enhance that of others. Bourguiba dozed and signed papers submitted to him, only to protest the following day—or forget the matter altogether.

As one Tunisian recalled later, "every morning we awaited news that yet another man appointed the day before would be relieved of his duties in a continuing struggle for influence in the palace. There was total political instability, the country seemed to be shrouded by dense fog."[1]

To understand better the motives that prompted a group of men backing the then minister of interior, Zine El Abidine Ben Ali, and urging him to take matters into his own hands, a glance at those traumatic days before November 7, 1987, is essential.

The drama leading to the predawn takeover by Ben Ali began on September 27, 1987, when the State Security Court (Tribunal de la Sûreté de l'État) reached its verdict in the trial of a group of Islamic militants. Some were sentenced to death, others to imprisonment, but in the case of their leader, Rachid Ghannouchi, there was insufficient evidence for the ultimate penalty. At least such was the argument of the presiding judge, Hachemi Zammel, who influenced the decision by three judges against two, thus sparing Ghannouchi the gallows. Some observers of that period claim that the interior minister (Ben Ali) also argued against capital punishment for the arch-fundamentalist.

The verdict was a blow to those men around Bourguiba who preached an all-out, uncompromising war on Islamic activists. Among them were Mahmoud Benhacine, considered at the time to be Bourguiba's closest adviser and confidant, and Mohammed Sayah, minister of education and scientific research. These two as well as several others who had easy access to the president and to his "éminence grise," Madame Sassi, immediately began scheming to have the verdict reversed.

Events gained momentum on October 2, when Bourguiba removed Rachid Sfar as prime minister and appointed Ben Ali in his place, satisfied with his performance as interior minister. At the same time, Mahjoub Ben Ali (no relation) became the head of the Destour Party, having proved himself as head of the party's militia, whose members had been involved in tracking down Muslim militants and, apparently, in some cases, had taken justice into their own hands. Such actions were opposed by Ben Ali who insisted on strict legality in all procedures. A man with Ben Ali's military and security training certainly did not want a "parallel" police running wild or substituting itself for the legal authorities.

Presumably unbeknownst to Bourguiba, his influential niece, Madame Sassi, disliked Mahjoub Ben Ali. She had had him removed on October 17, and replaced by Hamed Karoui, another long-standing member of the party.

On this confusing chessboard of palace rivalries and political scheming, the picture eventually became clear: the conflict was pitting Ben Ali against Sayah. The stakes were the Carthage palace and with it, obviously, Tunisia.

Sayah quickly moved to undermine Ben Ali's position and reputation by planting rumors of a planned coup to topple Bourguiba. Nonetheless Ben Ali continued functioning as prime minister, apparently unperturbed. Thus, On October 16 he announced measures in favor of poor farmers, and six days later proclaimed a fiscal amnesty and an increase in the minimum wage. All were within his mandate as prime minister.

Carrying out his official duties, on October 27 Ben Ali prepared a partial reshuffle of his cabinet, and duly submitted the list of his nominees to Bourguiba for approval. The president signed the list, but the following day he claimed that some ministers were too young—and he apparently forgot their names. He also had a tantrum when he saw that the name of the minister for economic planning was Mohammed Ghannouchi—nothing to do with the fundamentalist whose death he demanded despite the tribunal's verdict. Still, with a trembling hand he crossed the new minister's name from the list and, almost in the same breath, demanded a retrial for Rachid Ghannouchi with a guaranteed death penalty.

According to the vivid account of Bourguiba's last days in office in the well-informed French-language weekly *Jeune Afrique*,[2] Ben Ali as well as Justice Minister Mohammed Salah Ayari pleaded with Bourguiba that there was no legal grounds for such action as the case was already closed. Bourguiba left the room but, prompted by his intimate advisers, asked again for Ghannouchi's head on November 2. By then Ben Ali and a close associate who was to become his first prime minister, Hedi Baccouche, had become convinced that some form of action was essential. "The incoherent statements of the president had become catastrophic, pathological," *Jeune Afrique* reported.

On November 3 Bourguiba received visiting U.S. Senator George McGovern who praised the Tunisian president as "one of the greatest heads of state in the world."[3] Whether or not McGovern had been briefed by the U.S. Embassy in Tunis about the state of Bourguiba's health is not clear. It is certain that Ambassador Robert H. Pelletreau was perfectly aware of the Tunisian president's mental capabilities but for obvious diplomatic reasons did not necessarily state this bluntly to official visitors. Pelletreau certainly was very careful in describing the atmosphere in the Carthage palace to the author a few weeks before Ben Ali's takeover.

On the same day Bourguiba canceled his previous appointment of Tunisia's representative to the United Nations. No explanation was given. On November 4 the president demanded that the man he had named as head of the Destour Party on October 17 be immediately replaced. The problem was that the president had forgotten his name (Hamed Karoui). In a fit of pique, Bourguiba blamed his poor memory on Mahmoud Benhacine, the man who read the daily press to him every morning.

On the morning of November 5, Bourguiba summoned Ben Ali and told him to set a new trial for Rachid Ghannouchi and his accomplices for November 9. Apparently that was all that interested the old president, and Ben Ali decided, again according to *Jeune Afrique*, that "Bourguiba's mental capabilities were finished." Apparently he also learned that Mohammed Sayah, minister of education and scientific research, and his associates were planning to remove Ben Ali from office and throw him in jail. The race for the Carthage palace was reaching the finishing line.

For Ben Ali, the crucial factor was the support of the National Guard, a militarized police force formed along the lines of the French Gendarmerie Nationale. As in France, the Guard is used for the maintenance of order and security duties and does not have the role of city police, except in some rural areas. Together with Baccouche, Ben Ali contacted Habib Amar, the Guard's commander, informed him of the plan to remove the president and stressed the constitutional aspect, namely the pertinent paragraph (Article 57) stipulating the legality of such an act in the event of the president's incapacity to perform his functions. Amar agreed and, in the evening of November 7, late passersby and motorists in Tunis noticed the Guard's blue armored cars patrolling the streets.

Significantly, the army was informed but not asked to participate in the operation. A career soldier trained in French and U.S. military academies, Ben Ali did not want to involve the military in an internal problem that concerned the country's political rather than military establishment as well as the constitution. To him, the sole task of the armed forces was to defend Tunisia against external enemies.

The National Guard quickly took position around the usual key objectives, which could have unforeseen consequences in any form of sudden takeover: the radio and television stations, the main post office, the Ministry of the Interior, and the presidential palace, a massive structure surrounded by a white wall in one of the world's prime locations: near the ruins of ancient Carthage overlooking the blue Mediterranean. The presidential guards outside the palace gates handed over their weapons without protest and were replaced by the National Guard. Stage one of the scenario was completed swiftly and without a single sign of opposition.

Sayah and his close companions were arrested in their beds around 3:00 A.M. of November 7. Among them was General Ahmed Nooman, Air Force chief of staff and a nephew of Madame Sassi. Most of those arrested were taken to the National Guard barracks near the former airport of El Aouina. A number of other officials known for their strong support of Bourguiba were placed under house arrest.

The time now came to make the operation constitutional. Also about 3:00 A.M., an interior ministry official telephoned seven leading Tunisian doctors who had recently treated Bourguiba for his various ailments. (Bourguiba also occasionally consulted American, French, and Swiss doctors.) They included Dr. Mohammed Guediche, who treated Bourguiba during his heart attack in 1984, and a respected neurologist, Professor Abdelaziz Annabi. All were told to report promptly to the interior ministry on the Avenue Habib Bourguiba in the heart of Tunis.

The doctors were perfectly aware of the old president's mental and physical state—as were many other citizens of a country in which the leader's gaffes and incoherence were the fare of daily gossip. Together, the doctors signed a simple medical bulletin on a sheet of white paper without any printed heading. They did not examine the president before their action but apparently were convinced of its validity.

Dawn was breaking when Ben Ali and Baccouche, both in the interior ministry building, put the finishing touches to the statement the prime minister about to become president was to read on national radio. According to aides who witnessed the preparation of the text, Baccouche read and re-read the statement, paying attention to every dot and comma.

The event was of considerable importance, not only to Tunisia but to the rest of the world as well. Bourguiba was a well-known—and frequently admired—symbol of Tunisia's progressive and enlightened independence and the country's freedom from the usual Third World torment, military interference, and general decline. In fact, instead of declining, like most African and even Arab countries, Tunisia was advancing—and largely thanks to Bourguiba's initial vision of a new post-colonial world. Tunisia was also strategically important. The fact that in his last years in power the founder of modern Tunisia was not exactly "compos mentis," was not well known around the world. Equally underestimated in many diplomatic dispatches was the extent of Tunisia's economic and moral decline in the 1980s and the intrigue around the president in the twilight of his power.

Diplomats are not necessarily the best sources of accurate political information, in fact quite to the contrary. To cite one example: on the eve of Tunisia's nationalization of the land owned (or held) by French settlers in 1964, the U.S. embassy in Tunis sent an assessment categorically dismissing such a prospect.[4] The fact that the official who drafted the report saw his career come to a quick end does not excuse such blatant misunderstanding of a country into which the United States had poured well over a billion dollars (at the time of Ben Ali's takeover) and which, all things considered, was not that difficult to monitor. (The diplomat who had tried, unsuccessfully, to stop the controversial and misleading report was subsequently rewarded with an assignment in Chad and, then, with the ambassadorship to Togo.)

But Ben Ali's action was not something that the future president of Tunisia wanted to leave to diplomatic speculation or misinterpretation, especially in the embassy of a superpower which had excellent relations with Tunisia. More than nine years later, Pelletreau revealed to the Tunisian Arabic-language daily *Echourouk* that

I was informed very early, in the morning of November 7 [1987] by Mr. Baccouche, who had become prime minister. I immediately informed the authorities in Washington. The following day I was instructed by President George Bush to convey congratulations to President Ben Ali in which he [Bush] expressed his satisfaction that the change was carried out without any bloodshed.[5]

Indeed, not a drop of blood was shed as the new leader moved to secure his power. Before he announced his act to the country, he took special care to inform the man he was about to depose. Thus, at about 5:30 A.M., knowing Bourguiba's habits of early rising, Ben Ali telephoned the "grand monsieur" with the news. According to Tunisians who had reason to be familiar with that conversation, the old president replied, when told of Ben Ali's forthcoming radio announcement, "you are right, I should have thought of it before." Thus, in effect, ended the "Bourguiba era," without violence, "*à la tunisienne.*"

It was only after that conversation that Ben Ali was driven to the radio station, on the Avenue de la Liberté not far from the U.S. embassy, to make his brief takeover address. He ended his broadcast with the traditional "long live Tunisia, long live the republic." The announcement was over in four minutes, according to some of those who listened. The business of governing was about to begin—and it was going to be very different. According to several Tunisians interviewed subsequently, the country was emerging from the "fog" which had shrouded it for so long.

Almost at the same time, Dr. Amor Chadli, Bourguiba's personal physician, appeared at the gates of the palace for the regular morning visit to his patient. He was told, apparently politely, about what had happened and that the telephone to the palace had been cut. Dr. Chadli needed no further explanation and drove back to the Pasteur Institute not far from the radio station where Ben Ali had announced his decision to remove "according to the constitution" a president incapable of carrying out his functions. Dr. Chadli was at his desk in time to listen to the announcement that Hedi Baccouche had formed a new cabinet of 30 members—of whom only nine were new appointees.

At 3:00 P.M. Ben Ali was driven to the National Assembly building next to the famous Bardo museum where he was sworn in as Tunisia's second president. The fourth eldest child of 11 of a simple dockworker's family, he was dressed in his usual dark suit and black shoes. He was 51 years and two months old, and he was in power.

Meanwhile, still in his sprawling and ornate Carthage palace, Bourguiba refused to sign a document, prepared in advance, in which the founder of modern Tunisia would recognize his inability to govern. "Saida Sassi is in tears. . . . The former president does not want to leave Carthage and insists that he was betrayed," recorded the reliable *Jeune Afrique*.[6] Across Tunis, newspaper vendors shouted "extra, extra," as Tunisians snapped up 50,000 copies of the special edition of the French-language daily *La Presse*, which normally appears in the morning. The National Guard still surrounded the Carthage palace, normally the seat of power but which for the next 48 hours became a gigantic, gilded cage for a man who had overstayed his time.

After numerous and often stormy negotiating sessions, late in the morning of November 9, Bourguiba was taken by helicopter to nearby Mornag, site of one of his residential villas. His cooks, his servants, and Madame Sassi followed. And a Tunisian journalist concluded, "that man (Bourguiba) has reached the end of the road along which he carried his passion for power. He had become incapable of governing and Tunisia drifted with him, like a rudderless ship. There was no choice but to govern without him."[7]

Immediate reactions varied and included some spectacular headlines in France and the United States announcing a "coup," which was followed in the subsequent days by more careful analyses outlining the reasons for the takeover and its urgent necessity. *Newsweek*, which did not have to rush to press immediately, wrote:

Tunisia is clearly at a turning point, Bourguiba's health has been declining for years, and in recent months the aging, senile leader. . . . had grown increasingly erratic. Bourguiba's instability also threatened to exacerbate social tensions. The economy has faltered. Political life stagnated as Tunisians grew increasingly dissatisfied with the president's rule.

And, describing some reactions to Ben Ali in the West, the magazine concluded:

Western leaders were heartened. France quickly welcomed his (Ben Ali's) accession. Washington was quietly pleased. . . . However much Ben Ali may be liked in Washington or Paris, it's far from clear that he's the choice of Tunisia. He was just appointed, after all, by a man he declared non compos mentis.[8]

Perhaps alone amid the large diplomatic corps in Tunis, French Ambassador Jean Bressot insisted that "it was a coup d'état because Bourguiba did not agree." The reaction of the Foreign Affairs Ministry in Paris soon prompted the envoy to correct this analysis.

Britain's *Economist*, for unexplained reasons more frequently than not critical of Tunisia, wrote that although "the long reign of Mr. Habib Bourguiba as president of Tunisia seemed likely to end in disappointment and division," a "cleanly executed constitutional coup has left one of the Arab world's most sophisticated countries in a rare mood of optimism." In listing various measures planned by the new president, the respected conservative British weekly agreed that "he [Ben Ali] seems to mean it. New laws easing restrictions on political parties and the press are to be sent to parliament soon. . . . It is not yet clear how open to new ideas Mr. Ben Ali really intends to be."[9]

Describing Tunisia's economic problems at the end of the "Bourguiba era," the weekly concluded that

Mr. Ben Ali will not change the pro-Western policies of Mr. Bourguiba. The relaxed way in which Tunisians reacted to the end of 30 years' rule by one man was a tribute to Mr. Bourguiba's legacy of tolerance and relative sophistication, buttressed by the highest standard of education in North Africa. The new president went out of his way to remind Tunisians how much they owed to Mr. Bourguiba. Now the old man who once rejoiced in the title of "supreme combatant," and has been left with that of "leader to independence," will spend his remaining days honorably, in the gilded cage of one of the many palaces he built for himself."[10]

Perhaps the most apt political epitaph for the forcibly retired president was written in the London *Observer*, which thus summed up the situation in two terse albeit somewhat flippant sentences: "Tunisia today is like a family long dominated by a cantankerous relative which has finally plucked up the courage to put him in an institution. The principal feeling is relief: but there is also regret that the old man didn't chose to go with more dignity and on his own feet."[11]

On the whole, the West expected the new president to open the road to wider reforms and, at the same time, be more capable of containing militant Islam.

There was little doubt that, at least in the near future, Tunisia's destiny would be dominated by the Destour Party founded by Mr. Bourguiba, and by men who lived most of their political lives in the shadow of the "Supreme Combatant." The party has become a national institution rather than a political organization, penetrating every nook and cranny of Tunisian life.[12]

Indeed, although subsequently renamed the Constitutional Democratic Rally (French initials RCD), the party retained the entire Destour structure and most of its key organizers and "militants" (French term for activists).

The reaction of Tunisians themselves was reflected in the basically accurate Western press coverage: relief and expectation of a better and more coherent future. *Jeune Afrique*, that consistent chronicler of Tunisia's ups and downs since its independence, recorded some most poignant ones.

Habib Achour, the 77–year-old labor leader who often challenged Bourguiba and who had spent most recent years in jail and later under house arrest, was awakened by his wife with the news. "God does exist," he said with a sigh of relief.

Ahmed Mestiri, founder and head of the opposition Movement of Socialist Democrats (French initials MDS), also learned of the takeover, by a telephone call received while in bed. "I am not surprised," he was quoted as saying, "because for some time I believed that it was either Bourguiba or Ben Ali."

Mechir Khantouche, vice president of the National Assembly and member of the Destour Political Bureau, was in Tripoli, Libya, when a Syrian friend woke him up with the news. "I am not surprised, Tunisia needed a new man, now she has found him," were his words.

In Geneva, attending a meeting with foreign investors, Ismail Khelil, governor of the Central Bank, received the news by telephone from Abdelmajid Chaker, Tunisian ambassador to Switzerland. "Zine has got the palace," was the terse message. "God be praised," came the answer.

Years later, the radical transformation of the leadership from an ailing old statesman into a vigorous man anxious to project a new image of Tunisia was recorded by a Tunisian journalist who had accompanied both presidents during their state visits to Washington. In a memorandum addressed to the author of this study, the journalist, who insisted on anonymity, wrote:

On a glorious spring day in May 1990, on the south lawn of the White House, President Ben Ali was received with the full honors due a state visit. Although he had visited Washington privately in 1989 after addressing the U.N. General Assembly in New York, this was his first formal visit to the United States since his coming to power. The welcoming ceremony highlighted the rejuvenation of the Tunisian state.

For the blasé Washington politicians and journalists, there was nothing unusual about such a welcome. But for many members of the audience invited to the White House, and especially for the Tunisians who had attended previous Tunisian-American functions at the White House, there was indeed something dramatic and moving about the event they witnessed. It emphasized a sense of regained national dignity and self-respect.

In 1985, Habib Bourguiba, the first Tunisian head of state since independence, paid a visit to the White House. That visit left a different impression. Already in his eighties, Bourguiba displayed signs of old age and failing health. He remained seated while President Reagan delivered his farewell, standing. He even interrupted the American president in order to enquire, in French, about issues which he through President Reagan had omitted to mention. Bourguiba's speech was halting and slurred. Eventually, he had to be helped out of his seat by Mr. Reagan. By contrast, nearly six years later, Ben Ali delivered his remarks in his own language, Arabic, with the vigor and self-confidence of the leader who has just pulled his young nation from the brink.

The coming to power of Ben Ali also put an end to the pessimistic speculation about the future of Tunisia. Most experts had underestimated the regenerative capacity of the Tunisian body politic. Many were surprised by the peaceful transition which brought to the helm of Tunisia another moderate leader. Some, before 1987 and even a few years into the Change, did not expect Tunisia to overcome the fundamentalist challenge the way it did.

A much more spicy description of Bourguiba's last state visit to Washington was given by Howard and Gayle Radley Teicher in *Twin Pillars to Desert Storm:*

Although eighty five years old, Bourguiba showed no sign of voluntarily stepping down from presidency and remained relatively vigorous. In fact, we regularly received reports that, despite his age, Bourguiba continued to maintain a certain fondness for women other than his wife, a situation which led to frequent domestic quarrels and some significant political maneuvering by Madame Bourguiba. . . .

The president [Reagan] met privately in the Oval Office with President Bourguiba for thirty minutes and then joined the rest of the Tunisian and American delegations in the adjoining Cabinet Room for an exchange of views on regional and bilateral issues. . . . The discussions were conducted in both French and English with simultaneous interpretation provided by Sophie Porson, a senior State Department interpreter. Fifteen minutes into the meeting, President Bourguiba leaned across the table and exclaimed in French to Ms. Porson "If you were only fifteen years older and I were fifteen years younger, things might happen with us." Stunned by the outburst, Porson was speechless. Reagan and several others who did not understand French turned around to ask Ms. Porson what he had said, while those of us who understood gaped in awe. Porson blushed, mumbled something incomprehensible and Bourguiba returned to his monologue. However, two other times during the course of the Cabinet Room meeting he made similar comments to

Porson, which she was compelled to translate to the embarrassed amusement of the participants.[13]

In Tunisia itself, the hunted Islamists lay low during the next two days after Ben Ali's takeover, only to resume their tracts and inflammatory appeals. According to foreign assessments at the time, they believed that the takeover created a power vacuum which they hoped to fill. They were soon to be bitterly disappointed.

But, as pointed out before (see Chapter 4), the Islamists realized that, at least at the beginning of the new regime, it was in their interests to acknowledge Ben Ali's invitation for "national reconciliation" which followed the takeover. Thus some Islamic leaders praised the new head of state while others prepared to return from exile. The confrontation that, inevitably, took place afterwards was sufficiently described earlier in this study.

The ousting of Bourguiba also seemed propitious to other opposition groups that the former president had severely restricted. They included the Movement of Socialist Democrats (MDS) of Ahmed Mestiri, the Communist Party, and the small Progressive Socialist Rally. Although the MDS was the biggest opposition group, none of them had any impact on Tunisia's evolution in a country where the political scene was entirely dominated by the Destour Party. Still, no government could ignore their existence, particularly if it wanted to project the image of Tunisia as a democratic, multi-party society.

The three opposition parties began consultations in order to form a united platform in the face of the recent dramatic developments. While their talks went on, Mestiri received a telephone call from Abdelfattah Mourou, secretary general of the Islamic Tendency Movement (MTI), who was in exile and had been sentenced in absentia to ten years of forced labor by the State Security Court. Mourou said the MTI wanted to be included in the proposed united front, but Mestiri demanded a pledge that the fundamentalists renounce any recourse to violence. It was not clear whether Mourou made such a pledge but Mestiri was optimistic.

"Bourguiba was an obstacle to any political evolution," Mestiri, said after Ben Ali's takeover. He described the Bourguiba era as "the darkest period in Tunisia's history," and praised Ben Ali for being instrumental in sparing the lives of arrested Islamists. And he added: "We are now dealing with a serious man who knows what he wants and who is capable of achieving it provided he has the means." Mestiri stressed that if Ben Ali was serious about a real multi-party democracy, new general elections were needed as quickly as possible.[14]

But on November 12, Hedi Baccouche, the new prime minister, addressing some 100 Tunisian and foreign journalists in French, excluded the possibility of early elections. "The vote will take place at the expiration of the mandate of current legislature," he said. Still, the government had "not closed the door" to the idea of involving the opposition in the nation's life," Baccouche stressed.[15]

Bombarded by questions about the former president, Baccouche assured newsmen that "le leader Bourguiba" was "in good health, reading newspapers, watching television and reciting poetry, as usual." And, he concluded, "we have not forgotten someone who was a great man. The recent change has allowed us to keep a pure image of the fighter. We want to protect him from anything that would tarnish this image."

And this statement, basically, ended official comment about the fate of the founder of modern Tunisia, at least in the immediate future. The governmental *La Presse* carried exactly 13 lines on page 3 about Bourguiba's transfer to the Mornag residence and concentrated instead on the program of his successor.

For the Tunisian press, schooled in the cult of Bourguiba who demanded his pictures on the front pages virtually every day, the new prime minister had a word of advice that was to guide the behavior of journalists in the following years:

Journalists are free in the field of sports and brief news items ("*les faits divers*") but as far as politics are concerned there has always been a certain caution (pudeur). We would like to see an active participation by journalists in national thought as well as in calling the government's attention to the country's problems.[16]

The relatively detailed description of the events leading up to Bourguiba's ouster and its execution should allow the reader to have a better understanding of the situation as well as of the man who was to lead Tunisia in the years to come—Zine El Abidine Ben Ali. However, the picture would not be complete without mentioning the fate of some of the men whom the new regime considered to be partly responsible for the decay which accompanied Bourguiba's last years in power and thus had been harmful to the country.

Among those arrested in the early period that followed the takeover were Mohammed Sayah, minister of education and scientific research; Mansour Skhiri, former minister of housing and transport; and Mahmoud Benhacine, Bourguiba's loyal companion. All three were accused of exercising "harmful influence" on Bourguiba and of plans to sabotage the activities of the new government. The names of other persons apprehended would contribute little to this study. It should be pointed out, however, that Bourguiba's son, Habib Bourguiba, Jr., known to his friends as "Bibi," spent only a brief period under house arrest. In recent years, before Ben Ali's takeover, the younger Bourguiba had stayed out of politics and, in fact, was among the targets of his father's entourage influenced by Madame Sassi.

This relatively modest "housecleaning" completed, the new regime began looking at the situation inherited from the Bourguiba era and found three immediate priorities: (1) to halt the plunging living standards, (2) to face the threat of militant Islam, and (3) to deal with the difficult relations posed by Colonel Gadhafi's Libya. All three were dealt with by unusually efficient methods which eventually gave Tunisia the highest standard of living in the country's history, eliminated—or at least removed—the threat of Islamist extremism, and secured the safety of its borders.

Especially significant is the fact that during his first weeks in office, Ben Ali introduced a series of measures strengthening the country's legal code and framework and putting a strong accent on human rights. Thus, on November 26, 1987, the penal code was amended to limit the period for police custody and preventive arrest. On December 16, a special Constitutional Council was set up as a "watchdog" body over the application of the constitution. On December 29, the State Security Court was abolished and with it "emergency tribunals" dealing with offences of political nature. Also on the same day, the office of the General Prosecutor of the Republic was abolished "to strengthen the independence of the judicial system."[17]

Finally, on the year's last day (Tunisia observes the Western rather than Arabic calendar to facilitate contacts with the outside world), 405 convicted Islamic militants were given presidential pardons. In the course of the next few months, other measures of clemency were taken, and Amnesty International was authorized to establish an office in Tunis.

Amnesty International has always been highly critical of Tunisia's human rights record, even after Ben Ali's Change and despite various conciliatory measures toward the regime's opponents. In 1992 Amnesty claimed that "torture is still a systematic means of interrogation" in Tunisia—but then that self-appointed "guardian of the world's morality" has rarely been kind to any Third World country. Even the United States does not rate highly in its reports, which periodically speak of police brutality and the death penalty. In 1992 the Tunisian government admitted to some violations in the due process of law, undoubtedly caused by the tensions accompanying the struggle against Islamic extremists. At that time, a government official said 74 policemen were awaiting trial on charges of brutality against prisoners.[18]

On the whole, few assessments by various human rights groups took into account Tunisia's difficulties in dealing with what at one time was a wide-ranging assault on its government and institutions by Islamic militants. The fact that Tunisia basically lived in a state of siege to preserve a system applauded by much of the Western world did not often influence the sometimes strident criticism of its practices. For example, a report submitted by the State Department in January 1997, to the Committee on Foreign Relations of the U.S. Senate and the Committee on International Relations of the House of Representatives claimed that,

the [Tunisian] security forces continued to be responsible for serious human rights abuses. . . . The ability of citizens to change their government has yet to be demonstrated. Members of the security forces reportedly tortured and beat prisoners and detainees. Security forces also monitor the activities of government critics and at times harass them, their relatives, their associates. Prison conditions reportedly ranged from spartan to poor. . . . The Government generally did not respond effectively to allegations of human rights abuses, often not divulging the results of investigations. It demonstrated a pattern of intolerance of public criticism and continued to stifle freedom of speech, press and association.[19]

It should be noted that Amnesty International had relatively unhindered access to Tunisia, something a number of other countries have denied it. Thus, during the communist era, the human rights organization rarely reported on the situation in the Soviet Bloc countries. The report to the U.S. legislative bodies by the State Department was, in part, based on complaints by Tunisian opponents and on several occasions used the term "reportedly." The author was in no position to verify all its claims as opponents of the Tunisian regime appear to be wary of inquisitive foreigners. In any case, when this work was written, the overwhelming accent in the country was on economic achievements and the regime's progressive policies. The few opposition voices available basically offered no alternate program but merely appeared to want a "slice" of power—or all of it. Inevitably, such opponents resent the regime's efforts to limit their activities in a country that regards itself as vulnerable.

An official Tunisian publication on human rights (19) stated that

the number of alleged human rights abuses in Tunisia (e.g., for exceeding the legal period of pretrial incommunicado detention or for mistreatment) has dropped in recent years below the proportions observed in many countries where the protection of human rights is considered to be well developed. Every allegation is studied, on the principle that the respect of human dignity requires the protection of the dignity of every individual, . . . Furthermore, every time a case is raised in a communication from a United Nations mechanism . . . the Tunisian government makes the appropriate investigations and provides the requested answers, in the aim of establishing the truth.[20]

"It may be recalled," according to the text, "that Tunisia has ratified almost all international pacts and conventions, and that the country's constitution places these texts, once ratified, at the top of its legal hierarchy."

Discussing the issue of Islamic fundamentalism in the context of national security, the Foreign Ministry publication wrote,

The government's reaction following the rise of the fundamentalist movement in Tunisia in 1990 and 1991 has never been based on the security aspect, which was only an element that was necessary to protect the country from illegal acts and terrorist crimes. The Tunisian government counteracted the fundamentalists' strategy by applying the law, never resorting to a state of emergency or to exceptional justice. On the contrary, the greatest task was that of clearing the field that served for recruitment and the rooting out of fundamentalism, through a profound reform of the schools and by putting an end to the invasion of the mosques by false imams [Muslim clergymen] and extremist preachers.[21]

NOTES

1. Mustapha Khammari, director of *Dar Assaba* publishing company, in conversation with the author.

2. *Jeune Afrique*, November 1987.

3. Official statement at the Carthage palace.

4. Author's conversation with the diplomat who drafted the report.

5. *Echourouk*, 17 June 1997.

6. *Jeune Afrique*, November 1987.

7. Mohammed Habib Ladjimi in *Jeune Afrique*, November 1987.

8. *Newsweek*, 16 November 1987.

9. *The Economist*, 14 November 1987.

10. Ibid.

11. *The Observer*, 15 November 1987.

12. Author's dispatch in *The Washington Times*, 9 November 1987.

13. Howard and Gayle Radley Teichev, *Twin Pillars to Desert Storm* (New York: William Morrow, 1993), pp. 333–334.

14. Interview in the French daily *Le Monde*, 9 November 1987.

15. Ibid., 12 November 1987.

16. Transcript of the statement.

17. *Le Droit de L'Homme en Tunisie: Options et Réalisations*, p. 3.

18. Slaheddine Maaoui, at the time director of the Tunisian External Communications Agency, in conversation with the author.

19. Text of the State Department report.

20. *Reflections on Human Rights in Tunisia*, Human Rights Department, Ministry of Foreign Affairs, June 1996.

21. Ibid.

CHAPTER 6

A Nation in Step

The dense crowd that had massed on both sides of the street between the Lycée Technique and the seat of the local *gouvernorat* (province) waited for more than an hour. The atmosphere was that of a weekend outing. Pipes of amateur bands shrilled and drums kept up the beat. High-school girls giggled and some joked with the policemen and black-uniformed security troops lining the sidewalk at regular intervals, facing the assembled populace. Nearby, the massive walls of the 9th-century *ribat*, or fortress, added a historic dimension to a political fiesta in a Tunisian city.

The date was April 14, 1997, and Sfax, known as the capital of the south and Tunisia's second largest city, awaited a rare visitor: President Zine El Abidine Ben Ali. The "Sfaxis" are considered to be thrifty, hard working, persevering, and quite independent. A naval bombardment was required to subjugate them when the French colonial mandate was established in 1881.

From the beginning of his tenure as Tunisia's second president, Ben Ali has made a point of visiting a different province, or at least its seat, every few months. The operation is not as simple as it sounds. Tunisia's "democratic general," a term still occasionally used by the French press although he rarely, if ever, refers to his military rank, is one of the Arab world's most vulnerable leaders. He apparently is one of the top men on the "hit list" of Islamic terrorists trained in camps outside Khartoum and in Lebanon's Beka'a valley. He has immunized the country against fundamentalism and destroyed the structure of the Islamic movement in Tunisia, perhaps forever. According to reliable information, the leaders in charge of fundamentalist death squads have condemned Ben Ali to the ultimate punishment, perhaps believing that without him Tunisia would fall into their hands.

Consequently, security is not taken lightly by Ben Ali or his aides. In fact, it is paramount. While the president is well protected behind the walls of his Carthage palace and during an occasional public appearance in the capital, a "field trip" could easily offer an opportunity for a terrorist attack. Sfax was no exception.

During his seven hours in Sfax, an estimated 3,000 uniformed security personnel and civilian members of the RCD were deployed throughout the city of 700,000. Sharpshooters took positions on rooftops around the area he was to visit. In the abandoned waterfront industrial zone, soon to be converted into a playground, men lined the coastline, looking out toward the sea. Equally protected were the streets through which his motorcade traveled. Clearly, Ben Ali has not wasted his security training.

He arrived by plane at the airbase near the city and was driven to its heart, for a 600-yard walk, a security nightmare. Before his bullet-proof car reached the square where the walk was to start, a small bus screeched to a stop, spilling out black-uniformed, helmeted security guards. They accompanied the president's every step, amidst the deafening chant "Ben Ali— Tunis, Ben Ali—Tunis." While the crowds most definitely had had to be organized to welcome the visitor, foreign reporters watching the show were convinced of the spontaneity of the greeting.

Less certain was whether Ben Ali enjoyed the acclaim or whether he felt it his duty to show himself to the people and acknowledge their obvious enthusiasm and beaming faces. The author has seen many rallies in Arab countries, but only the ones staged for Egypt's Gamal Abdel Nasser had a similar degree of unprompted expression of approval. But while Nasser and Bourguiba thrived on mass demonstrations, Ben Ali gave the impression of merely carrying out his job.

He walked slowly, periodically clasping his hands over his head to acknowledge the deafening chant, A stocky man of average height, with a square face and jet black hair, he wore his usual dark suit, white shirt, tie with a matching breast pocket handkerchief, and black shoes. Close to him walked two men carrying what looked like attaché cases. In fact, they were portable protective shields, one of the latest gadgets in modern-age security, to be erected instantly by a push-button mechanism. Nothing, but absolutely nothing, was left to chance.

There were no impromptu handshakes—too dangerous. Petitions and letters to the president handed from the crowd were collected by an aide. Ben Ali did kiss girls in national costume who stepped forward and pelted him with rose petals as the drums continued to roll.

"Look, very few chechias," an official said, pointing to the red, soft pillbox caps Tunisians have worn for years. "During Bourguiba's rule, there were many more." Indeed, the applauding and cheering mass was dressed mainly in European attire. There were few flowing robes. Many schoolgirls in the crowd wore jeans.

In the spanking clean, new building housing the provincial administration, the president was asked to greet the local "notables,"—heads of enterprises, lawyers, physicians, educators, members of the administrative apparatus. Most wore Western suits, but there were some, usually elderly, men in brown *djeebas* and red *chechias*. The women—about a score—wore European dress. Patiently, he shook some 300 hands as the long line advanced up the stairs to the large room where he waited. A few remarks were exchanged, and there was a smile or two, but on the whole the atmosphere was serious.

After a brief break and the departure of the city's elite, Ben Ali put on his glasses and opened what was described as a working session with the members of the local "general council," which normally includes mayors and key administrators of a province. About 50 men and two women sat behind desks set up in several semicircular rows. Several made brief speeches thanking him for coming to Sfax. There was some scattered applause. When the governor, resplendent in a ceremonial black suit with silver epaulettes and frogging on the sleeves, launched into a long panegyric, Ben Ali interrupted, saying, "let's talk about the region's problems one by one. For example, let's start by the issue of drinking water."

Several terse reports followed, and at one stage Ben Ali turned to the minister of economy, present in the room, for the government's comment.

Electricity supplies to villages as well as the problems of neglected rural areas, the so-called "zones of darkness" or "shadow zones," were mentioned. Ben Ali interrupted periodically, consulting a file in front of him. He stressed, in clipped tones, the need to increase the city's health facilities, improve the entrance to the local natural park, and speed up the work on a modern sewer system. He remarked that the city needed an open-air theater and "perhaps it should have been built before the new provincial headquarters"—the brand new building where he was speaking. He warned the assembled representatives of the regional authority to improve a dangerous curve on the road toward Tunis, where an accident had taken place the day before. "Take care of it by the end of the year," he said in a tone that left no room for doubt that he meant it. The pertaining ministers present in the room took copious notes.

In contrast to the often verbose and chaotic atmosphere of similar meetings in most Arab countries, the performance was incredible. The meeting was brisk, to the point, and there was no doubt that Ben Ali was familiar with the issues he had come to discuss. He had done his homework and it showed. No one smoked; those who intended to ask questions or make statements had to first raise their hands. As one of his ministers said earlier, "Ben Ali maintains an exceptional rhythm of work. We have a political leader who has succeeded in making people work. Those in the government who are lazy or negligent don't last long."[1]

The day's schedule included the inauguration of a branch of the Central Bank, a tour of some abandoned industrial areas, a visit to a factory making couscous (semolina) for export, as well as of the installations of British Gas, drilling in the sea off Sfax. All this required time, and something had to be cut short. In Ben Ali's case it was the elaborate four-course meal for the president, his suite, and invited guests under a giant tent set up near the governor's residence. A team of waiters rushed to ladle out an excellent fish soup (local specialty), then quickly change plates to serve fish couscous (a Tunisian specialty), but there was little time for fruit and sweet cakes. The whole meal lasted barely 45 minutes. The singer in the band serenading the visitor was given no time to perform. Ben Ali was working and so were all those with him.

Few outside Tunisia knew much about the man who succeeded Bour-guiba and proceeded in a no-nonsense manner to "make people work," even though ten years after the Change a number of government departments were crippled by inertia and inefficiency. He is one of 11 children of a dockworker in Hammam-Sousse, south of Tunis. Upon completion of his secondary education, Ben Ali joined the army and undertook higher military training, first in a special staff college at St. Cyr in France, then, in the artillery school at Chalons-sur-Marne (now called Chalons-en-Champagne) also in France, and finally studied intelligence and security training at Fort Holabird, Maryland, and anti-aircraft artillery training at Fort Bliss, Texas. At the same time, he managed to obtain a diploma in electronic engineering.[2]

Thus equipped, he proceeded to set up, in 1964, a Military Security Directorate at the Tunisian Defense Ministry, an organization he directed for the following ten years. He served for a period as military attaché in Spain and Morocco and in 1977 was named general director of national security in Tunis. In 1980 he left as ambassador to Poland, at that time a country still firmly in the Soviet-led Warsaw Pact. According to one official biographer, "he spent four years penetrating the mysteries of diplomacy to promote Tunisia, working with unquenchable devotion." Somehow, such lurid prose (presumably the result of a translator's enthusiasm) does not fit a man as precise and businesslike as Ben Ali.

Back in Tunis again, in 1985 he became minister for national security, and then, on April 26, 1986, minister of the interior. The same year, with Bourguiba still in power, Ben Ali entered the Political Bureau of his Socialist Destour Party as assistant secretary general. On October 2, 1987, on his 51st birthday, Ben Ali was prime minister. Two months and five days later, he was sworn in as president.

His first year in office was marked by a number of events, some of them exceptionally significant for Tunisia but little known abroad. Seen from the outside world, Tunisia was still a long way from the kind of democracy practiced in Western countries and considered by them to be the only model, regardless of the different circumstances, traditions, and problems in various Third World countries. In short, the West expects every developing nation to emulate it in every respect, without transition or attenuating circumstances.

Sadok Chaabane, former minister of justice, believed that in November of 1987 "Ben Ali took over a regime in agony. At that time there was only bitter rivalry between the groups struggling without scruple to take over the heritage of a man unable to control the situation under the burden of his age."[3] While praising Bourguiba's enormous achievement in leading Tunisia to independence and setting the basis for its development, Chaabane believes that his reforms were superficial: "He liberated the country without liberating the people; he created institutions without giving them a soul. . . . He monopolized all decisions within the framework of 'personal power' and he presided over a bureaucracy more and more distant from the people's problems."[4]

Ben Ali's takeover methods illustrated how scrupulously he was committed to legality—even to the point of obtaining a medical certificate to remove a senile president. His subsequent months in office showed he intended to continue this approach, codifying every measure or asking, in some cases, for parliamentary approval (which was never refused).

A glance at some measures taken in 1988 shows considerable effort by the new president to make himself "as democratic as possible." However, Ben Ali was careful to reduce the risk of an uncontrolled political outburst, something that has never happened in Tunisia, a country by then accustomed to the system of "presidential democracy."

Some dates and events in 1988 are worth noting:

March 18—The opposition press received amnesty for what was called "press-related offenses," namely criticism of the regime.

April 8—Government employees fired for trade union activities, which were banned by Bourguiba, were re-instated.

April 12—Amnesty International received permission to open an office in Tunis.

May 3—A law governing the establishment of political parties was enacted. It led subsequently to the creation of the Progressive Socialist Rally, of the Social Party for Progress and of the Unionist Democratic Union.[5]

November 6—The Tunisian League for Human Rights announced that there were no longer "prisoners of conscience" in Tunisia.

From the Tunisian perspective, two major events marked the year as Ben Ali maneuvered to consolidate his power and lay the groundwork for a durable regime. One was the creation, on July 31 of the Constitutional Democratic Rally (RCD) which replaced the Socialist Destour Party, and the other was the signing of the National Pact, which brought together all legally recognized political parties, significantly on the first anniversary of the Change (November 7).

There were several reasons for the transformation of Bourguiba's old party into a new political force. The foremost among them was the government's need to use the vast party apparatus to implement its policies. In order to achieve that, the party needed a different ideology to suit a different style of government. The transformation took place at the last congress of Destour, which, in Tunisia's stilted official terminology, became known as "The Congress of Salvation." In convoking the Congress, Ben Ali asked that it be "authentically decisive," and put the stamp of approval on the fact that "we have definitely broken away from the negative aspects of the past and from the mentality of the one-party system."[6]

While the old party was "a party of independence," the new one became "a party for the president and for the Change" and was to lead Tunisia into the 21st century. Basically, it inherited the entire structure of Destour and its accoutrements, lock, stock, and barrel. Just as Destour was Bourguiba's essential tool, the RCD became Ben Ali's main power base.

Describing the "facelift" of the old party (Socialist Destour Party), Abdelaziz Ben Dhia, secretary general of its successor, said simply: "Socialism was no longer fashionable and the new president had different views."[7]

The new party—with Destour organizers, offices, typewriters, and printing presses—was immediately faced with a problem: should it be representing Tunisia's elite or should it become a movement embracing all social strata. The latter option—certainly a more democratic concept—prevailed. All Destour workers—"without exception," Ben Dhia stressed—were simply transferred to the new party. There were some structural changes and a new charter. The essential difference, again according to Ben Dhia, was that "the rank-and-file became essential in decision-making. The party accepted, for the first time, to contribute to the democratic development of society."[8]

The party structure consisted of 7,500 cells with varying numbers of members. A congress was to be held every five years. The key decisions on "options and orientation" were to be made by Ben Ali himself.

A congress would group between 2,400 and 2,500 delegates, elected by the rank-and-file. The first congress, in 1993, approved Ben Ali's major policy and economic decisions, including partnership with Europe and the necessary economic restructuring. The party stipulated, again conforming to the president's wishes, that state interference in the economy was inevitable in the initial stage because Tunisia was still a developing country.

The congress also decided that the rank-and-file would choose three candidates for each of the 144 seats in the Chamber of Deputies allotted to the party. The remaining 19 seats were earmarked for the opposition, to be divided on a nationwide basis according to the results of the vote. The congress confirmed the RCD's key role as that of "a framework party" (*parti de l'encadrement*) which "participates in Tunisia's political and economic transformation to reach an international competitive level."[9] The party has thus become the dominant political force in Ben Ali's new grand design. The role reserved for the opposition was that of limited criticism, provided that it was constructive. Such reasoning was based on the premise that Tunisia's form of democracy was still fragile and required considerable "apprenticeship."

Bourguiba's successor has thus created perfect conditions for the success of his program, with a minimum of interference by opposition forces. In fact, the authorized opposition parties have contented themselves with praising Ben Ali's policies while stipulating the need to "renovate the political landscape." Years later, Mohamed Harmel, head of the ex-communist Ettajdid Party, said he, as well as most opposition members, believed that "the national consensus" was essential if the country was to develop as fast as the international circumstances required.[10]

As Ben Ali's mandate approached its tenth anniversary, leaders of the "legal" opposition parties appeared to be impressed with his success in stemming the Islamic tide and improving Tunisia's economy. To quote Harmel again, "Tunisia has resolved Bourguiba's succession, has stopped the Islamic threat and has drafted economic solutions. To achieve more progress, it needs stability."[11] It was clear that such opposition as was allowed was not likely to hinder Ben Ali's program. In the words of an American diplomat, "the opposition parties have been co-opted." In short, the political spectrum has been narrowed to those who support Ben Ali's policies. The conditions of the system were not propitious for the creation of more militant forces, which, in any case, were unlikely to gain the support of the masses.

According to Chaabane, for more than 30 years Tunisia was dominated by a "political culture" based on a one-party system and the sequels of such a culture were not easy to overcome. "Ben Ali has frequently studied the problem involved in the transition from a single to a multi-party system," he wrote. "He is perfectly aware of the fact that three decades have embedded the one party system into Tunisia's political life and that any elimination of its consequences demands time and effort."[12]

Furthermore, Chaabane points out that within the ruling party

the absence of competition progressively creates a mentality of dependence upon the government, opportunism, and the absence of scruples to circumvent the law when occasion arises. As for the opposition, it also is affected by a similar mentality, becoming reconciled with the state and limiting itself to waiting for such initiatives as the state consents to grant it.[13]

Chaabane believes that, in such a political atmosphere, it has not been possible "to satisfactorily develop a culture of competition based upon initiative, independence, concern to show a difference by specific programs or the development of slogans."

At this stage, Chaabane concludes, "the moderate democratic opposition is neither structured nor prepared to lead the masses, rationalize its demands, or prepare alternate choices. The democratic forces are not yet ready." Consequently, he says, the "transitional stage requires that the path to change be controlled in order to prevent extremist movements seizing any opportunity to win over the dissatisfied."

With such factors in mind, Ben Ali obtained, on November 7, 1988, the signatures of all authorized opponents of the National Pact, a contract committing them to work together for the betterment of Tunisia. The contract stipulates that democracy based on "pluralism of opinions" is irreversible and guarantees "respect for differing opinions," protects minority rights, calls on all Tunisians to be loyal citizens, and proclaims the country's commitment to Islam and Arabism, "at the same time remaining open to other languages and civilizations." The legalistic president thus had a formal charter upon which he was to base his wide-ranging reforms.

And indeed, reforms followed, particularly in the field of human rights, although Ben Ali's record continued to be criticized by Amnesty International and, obviously, by his fundamentalist opponents. On January 25, 1989, the Tunisian president received the Louis Michel Democracy and Human Rights Prize, awarded by the French Institute for Political and Social Studies. A month later, a law was enacted abolishing the penalty of hard labor and commuting all such sentences to simple prison terms. On March 23, 1989, the Arab Institute for Human Rights set up its headquarters in Tunis.

To test the country's political temperature under the new regime, early legislative and presidential elections were held on April 2, 1989. The presidential vote was hardly more than a formality, as Ben Ali was the only candidate—just as Bourguiba had been in 1959 before he declared himself president-for-life. In Ben Ali's case, the elections formally began his first five-year term in office, the initial period after the takeover being considered transitional.

The somewhat complicated parliamentary electoral method at that time was based on a "constituency system" which clearly favored the dominant party, the ex-Destour in its new form of the RCD, which won 79.75 percent of the vote and all seats at stake. The six parties that formed the so-called "democratic opposition" obtained slightly less than 6 percent and no seats, and candidates running as independents obtained 14.6 percent. The "independents" were mostly camouflaged Islamic activists of the banned al-Nahda party or its sympathizers, and the degree of their support, while not directly threatening the regime, caused considerable concern to the establishment. According to Michael Collins Dunn,

The real story of the elections was not the winners but the performance of the al-Nahda supporters running as independents. . . . The al-Nahda movement had shown its strength, had flexed its muscles within the existing constitutional system and shown its ability to draw votes. It is true that it won no seats, and that it remained formally barred from political life, but it was clearly tolerated and permitted to function, and even run candidates.[14]

A government official said subsequently that "even the relatively strong showing disappointed the al-Nahda leaders, who had banked on a ground-swell [sic] of support. Short of that, they opted for a different strategy."

Sadok Chaabane feels that the vote

represented a bench test for the evaluation of the weight of political parties as well as of the potential of the new party in power after the Change. . . . The results were hardly satisfying for the Head of State because they did not introduce pluralism in the Chamber of Deputies. He thus ordered an amendment to the Electoral Code which guaranteed the presence of the democratic opposition in the Chamber. The amendment was approved December 27, 1993.[15]

It kept the system of "party lists," with the list obtaining the majority of votes within a given electoral district (*circonscription*) getting all parliament seats earmarked for that district. The remaining votes across the nation were to be divided among other parties. Under such a system, the number of parliamentary seats is higher than the seats at stake in the electoral districts, or 144 under the latest law. With a total of 163 members of the Chamber, the remaining 19 seats are divided among the losers of the various voting districts.

The new system was used in the March 20, 1994, parliamentary elections, in which the Democratic Socialist Movement (MDS) obtained ten seats, Ettajdid four seats, Unionist Democratic Union (UDU) three seats, and the Party for a Popular Union (PUP) two seats. Predictably, the RCD won a majority in all electoral districts and, thus, all 144 Chamber seats at stake. To Ben Ali and the men around him, the new Chamber represented a considerable improvement and another step in Tunisia's "democratic apprenticeship." Ben Ali himself was re-elected for another term in a parallel presidential vote—again unopposed.

Foreign critics of the Tunisian system were still unconvinced about Tunisian democracy, which did not conform to that of well-established Western concepts. And here perhaps the best explanation was offered by a Tunisian journalist, who said,

We're not advanced enough for the luxury of complete democracy. The big question is what should come first, democracy or economic development? The world must give us time to carry out our evolution. We have achieved something unique: we have peace and people don't have to worry about their kin not coming home at night.[16]

Nonetheless, at least until mid-1997, the U.S. Embassy in Tunis regarded the opposition parties as "co-opted" by the regime rather than representing a real challenge or a political alternative. Statements by opposition politicians generally reflected a docile attitude ("constructive" in official terminology) and, while praising the regime's achievements since Ben Ali's takeover, merely expressed the hope for a broader multi-party representation in parliament and in municipal councils.

A typical view was that of Mohamed Belhadj Amor, secretary general of the Party for a Popular Union (*Parti de l'Unité Populaire*), who praised Ben Ali's reforms and the first steps toward a wider political spectrum as "necessary conditions answering the people's aspirations for freedom, sovereignty and justice."[17] Consequently, he said,

the opposition parties have agreed to participate in the building of national cohesion and in the process of democratization and dynamism. . . . In my mind, the gradual approach adopted since the Change as far as democratization is concerned was necessary. It helped Tunisia avoid the shocks unhappily experienced by other countries.

Shortly before the 1994 elections, in a statement before the House of Representatives Foreign Affairs Committee, Robert H. Pelletreau, assistant secretary of state for Near Eastern Affairs and former ambassador to Tunisia, said Tunisia's electoral code "offers the real prospect of opposition party representation." Furthermore, Pelletreau continued,

In Tunisia we can see the fruits of our successful assistance programs. Tunisia has now reached the point at which it can offer assistance and training to less developed countries. . . . As a trendsetter in successful economic reform, Tunisia has established a standard which other countries seek to duplicate.[18]

By then the fundamentalist threat appeared to be minimal. Tunisia was developing and paying its foreign debt promptly. It was praised by the International Monetary Fund and the World Bank. It was poised for an association treaty with the European Union which was signed a year later. Its troublesome neighbors—Algeria and Libya—did not perturb Tunisia's development. Oussama Romdhani, at that time a diplomat in the Tunisian embassy in Washington, thus described the feeling of the ruling circles:

Tunisia has turned its back on fundamentalism. Our economic achievements deny demagogues any credibility. There is no constituency of despair. People are aware that fundamentalism is a threat, not a blessing and appreciate the peace and progress which came under Ben Ali. We know that we live in a rough neighborhood.[19]

The validity and nature of the electoral system clearly preoccupied Ben Ali and his close advisers who were determined to show the outside world—as well as the local constituency—that Tunisia's "democratic apprenticeship" was, indeed, evolving. In a speech which has become a form of guideline, at least for the first part of the second decade of the Change, the Tunisian president admitted before a selected audience in the Carthage palace on November 7, 1997, that the results of the last elections "have shown that the traditional electoral systems, including the proportional, do not meet our needs at the present stage in our political transformation." Consequently, he announced that the polling method for the Chamber of Deputies was to be "reinforced so as to enable the opposition to occupy a minimum of approximately 20 percent of the total number of seats" in the legislature.

This was to be accomplished, according to the official text of the speech, "by increasing the number of seats allotted to the national level, while the number allotted to the districts will remain approximately stationary despite the population increase, reaffirming our determination to give still greater impetus to plurality in parliament."[20]

By the end of 1997, Ben Ali felt that, at least for the time being, he had gone far enough in facilitating the activities of the "legal opposition." As he put it to the author's question submitted in writing, "from there on, it is up to the political parties to work in order to expand their audience."

Pointedly, he stressed that he saw no threat to his own ruling party, the RCD, which he described as "a majority party (which) without doubt, will remain as such for a long time, particularly as it enjoys very large mass support and has frequently demonstrated the ability to evolve and develop its message and its audience."[21]

The Carthage palace 10th anniversary speech—broadcast on state radio and television and reprinted in full in the press the following day—contained another indication of what Ben Ali's advisers call "the path to plurality." Presumably embarrassed by the fact that in two successive presidential elections Ben Ali was unopposed, the Tunisian leader hinted that the next vote—in 1999—would see a "method that will, at least during a period of transition, make it possible to increase the number of candidates standing for the office of President of the Republic." Officials speculated that two or more members of the "legal opposition" would offer their candidacies. Needless to say, Ben Ali had no fears of being defeated for what, under the constitution, would be his third and last mandate. (The constitution specifies that a president can stand twice for re-election.)

Ten years after he ousted Bourguiba from power, Ben Ali was unquestionably a highly popular president. Even progressive French newspapers, a priori hostile to the Tunisian president because of his clearly conservative leanings, speculated that in any completely free electoral contest Ben Ali could easily get 70 percent of the vote.

As he celebrated the anniversary, Ben Ali appeared to have a strong sense of his mission as Tunisia's "savior" from political and economic catastrophe. Recalling the event, he said:

From the beginning of my appointment as Prime Minister, I was able to realize the extent of the catastrophe which threatened the country. The situation was due to the bankruptcy of the policies pursued at that time, the paralysis of the state machinery, the resignation of the private sector and the disappointment of the population.

Thus the first task of the Change of 7 November 1987 was to re-establish the confidence of the state in itself and between the state and the population, in order to extricate the country from stagnation and threats of all kinds, particularly the fundamentalist threat, and to launch the necessary reforms. . . . It was also necessary to carry out a radical reform of the mental outlook, including a complete revamping of the educational system, of professional training and scientific research.[22]

Ben Ali, "the man who made the Tunisians work," follows an exacting and rigid schedule. Punctual and demanding, he believes in the economy of words and strict formality in conducting government business. Despite his numerous state visits across the globe, he is little known as a person. The glowing official biographies distributed by the government are just about as much insight into his personality as one is likely to get. With rare exceptions, he shuns the foreign press. He is said to trust a number of advisers and ministers, but, in the end, all major decisions are his. Ordinary Tunisians—his principal constituency—rarely see him except during his periodic official visits to outlying areas (such as the one to Sfax) or unannounced inspections of hospitals, schools, factories, or work sites. Party workers and government officials are invited to an occasional rally, usually in a covered stadium, where, after a series of deafening cheers led by party workers, Ben Ali reads a topical speech which rarely lasts more than 20 minutes. (Bourguiba used to speak for hours, mostly without any prepared text.) Security is always tight and the black-uniformed presidential guards stand by at the ready. Foreign diplomats point out that there is always a distance between Ben Ali and the first ranks of his audience.

The Carthage palace has changed since Bourguiba was "invited" to make room for his successor. New electronic security installations have been constructed, including a powerful barrier of massive steel rods on the road to the working annex, which is lowered when a visitor is cleared by security guards. The presidential guard has been reinforced by a contingent of soldiers, frequently seen doing pushups and other exercises in palace grounds. Anti-aircraft missiles protrude over the rooftops of the vast compound. Islamic fundamentalists have been silenced, but a man of Ben Ali's experience takes no chances. In fact, the president's palace has become a fortress.

Officials try to minimize this aspect of their "presidential democracy" by saying that under Ben Ali "a new executive complex has been built to accommodate the palace advisers and staff. The days of whimsical or improvised decisions are gone. All decisions are examined and checked thoroughly."

Officials summoned to see the president have to leave their cars in a special parking lot and are then driven to the entrance in palace cars or mini-buses. The same system applies when Ben Ali addresses groups of people. It works smoothly. A security system, "to accommodate outside visitors," often involves lengthy telephone calls by guards, while visitors remain in their cars outside the gate.

Cabinet meetings in the palace are usually held twice a month. In Bourguiba's days, they were informal gatherings, with ministers trickling in leisurely, sipping coffee or sweet mint tea, and privately sorting out various problems before sitting down around a table for more formal discussions. If one believes the monthly *Afrique Magazine*, all that changed shortly after Bourguiba's departure.

The meeting of the council of ministers starts punctually at 10:00 A.M. The magazine wrote:

The ministers are asked to arrive not more than five or maximum ten minutes before. They are ushered into a large rectangular conference room as ceremonial guards present their sabres in a formal salute. Once inside, the ministers have little time to talk to each other . . . at 10 o'clock the usher announces "the President of the Republic." Ben Ali enters, followed by the prime minister with whom he will have consulted before the meeting. Several accredited journalists as well as a television camera team follow.

 Every minister receives the agenda a week before and must be thoroughly familiar with it. Each minister who intends to speak has to submit an outline of the subject in advance to the palace secretariat and the president's adviser in this particular field. Frequently, slides projected on a large screen are used to illustrate problems under discussion. Apparently Ben Ali does not like to see ministers read from texts, their heads bowed. Ben Ali asks many questions, wants to know the precise reason for the decision suggested, and then opens the floor to discussion. Above all, he demands brevity. The more concise and to the point a minister is, the more his suggestion is likely to receive the president's attention. Even though a meeting can sometimes last up to three hours, no one smokes and no coffee or even water is served. All sessions are conducted in Arabic, although occasionally the French language is used as well.[23]

In addition to such highly regimented, formal meetings, from time to time Ben Ali meets various ministers in a more relaxed atmosphere. Such meetings vary in length and depend on the nature of the business at hand. The ministers are typical of Tunisia's elite: highly educated and perfectly bilingual (Arabic and French) and now under "presidential pressure" to learn English. Some already speak it fluently. For example, Habib Ben Yahia, minister of national defense, has a diploma in international relations from Columbia University. He served in various posts in the Foreign Ministry in Tunis before becoming ambassador to the United Arab Emirates in 1976, subsequently ambassador to Japan and South Korea, in 1984 to Belgium and then the United States. In 1991 he became minister of Foreign Affairs, a post he held until January 1997 when he became minister of National Defense.

Abdelbaki Hermassi, minister of Culture, is another fluent English speaker, with a Ph.D. from the University of California at Berkeley in 1971. He subsequently taught at Berkeley and did research at Princeton, served as Tunisia's envoy to the United Nations Educational, Scientific, and Cultural Organization (UNESCO) and wrote a number of studies, mainly on North African subjects. Unlike most ministers, Hermassi is not a member of the governing party.

Those who have seen the inner sanctum of the Carthage palace, Ben Ali's private study, describe an impressive array of computer consoles and stacks of diskettes. A trained electronic engineer, Ben Ali is apparently fascinated by computer technology and is linked directly to the networks of the interior and defense ministries.

Of Ben Ali's personal life not much is known except that he is married and the father of five children, including three grown daughters. His family does not appear to play a public role and is rarely seen with him at official functions. He is fastidious in his personal appearance and, on occasion, has been known to tell officials to shave better. He rises early and spends an hour or two in his private gymnasium.

One facet of Tunisia's life so far unaffected by Ben Ali's Change is the country's daily press. Just as it applauded everything Bourguiba said or did, it continues to laud every step and statement by his successor. Ben Ali's pictures are virtually daily front-page fare—and without much photographic imagination. Thus the president is seen sitting stiffly receiving a foreign dignitary, shaking hands with another, or talking to an official from behind his desk. A typical headline in the government French-language daily *La Presse* on April 4, 1997, was "Admirable work is being accomplished in Tunisia under the direction of President Ben Ali." Other headlines announce "International consecration of President Ben Ali's actions," "Pledge of workers to double their efforts in the face of the economic challenge," "Tunisia gives an example in Euro-Mediterranean cooperation," and many other similar jewels of official journalism.

It is not quite clear to what extent such a subservient form of journalism is inspired by the president himself or by courtiers and aides eager to please him. He certainly does not oppose it—or would have stopped it a long time ago. At a meeting with newspaper publishers in 1996 and in subsequent statements, Ben Ali showed some impatience with the "slow pace" of the transformation of Tunisian journalism. Still, in the year that followed there were no signs of significant change. Tunisian journalists, who privately laugh at their own product, are slow to leave a habit of long years—first under Bourguiba and now under Ben Ali. Apologists for such a form of journalism claim that in an Arab country it is essential to give strong support to the leader, particularly a popular and progressive one. But given Tunisia's level of education and proximity to Europe, it would seem that a more lively press would be more suitable. Most foreign visitors are struck by the monotony and subservience of the press which, unfortunately, often resembles the organs of the communist era in Russia. Glasnost has done away with that terminally boring press but Tunisia's Change is yet to act in this field.

Ten years after the Change, Tunisia's newspapers remained moribund, with journalists to a great extent practicing self-censorship. On the whole, newspapers generally took the cue from the official Tunisian news agency (*Tunis Afrique Presse*—TAP). Pictures of Ben Ali were ubiquitous. Editorials were careful, and criticism was extremely cautious and generally limited to economic issues. Journalists themselves joked about their *langue de bois*—wooden tongues—but little was being done to change it.

During 1997 there were some indications that the discerning Tunisian reading public was abandoning the local press in favor of imported newspapers, mainly French. No detailed information on this sensitive subject was readily available, but if the circulation was indeed falling, it should have been a clear signal about the quality of local journalism. The government claims that some 600 foreign publications are available in the country and that, in the second half of 1997, all universities and research institutes were to be connected to the Internet.

Apparently convinced by his aides and foreign critics that the ossified media did little to improve Tunisia's image as a budding democracy, Ben Ali decided to appeal to the press to join the other sectors more actively participating in the Change.

In the fall of 1997, the State Secretariat of Information was eliminated as not befitting a progressive country and giving the impression of government-sponsored information policy. In his hour-long speech on the 10th anniversary of his takeover, the Tunisian President said "we rely on media professionals to be conscientious and mature in placing their profession above all the temptations that are associated with it, numerous as they are in the world of the press." And he added:

As we embark upon a new decade it is normal that we should hope, in the next stage, to have a well-developed, bold press capable of creation, innovation and constructive criticism, at a time when the rate of production must be accelerated in every area. Information is a mission of civilization and a field in which competition is lively in this era of globalization and expansion into space.[24]

In what was an implicit criticism of the performance of the media during the period of other, more progressive changes, Ben Ali cautioned that "as we renew our appeal to those responible for press enterprises to seek quality, develop the media discourse so that it can reach a remarkable level, and approach issues honestly, audaciously and responsibly, professionals in this field no longer have any excuse to evade their responsibilities or resort to the easy way out by practising self-censorship."[25]

At this writing it was too early to assess the impact of such an unprecedented appeal. As one Tunisian newspaper publisher observed at the time, "At least it is now black on white but let's see who will take the risk first."

Tunisians are avid readers, and there are five Arabic- and two French-language dailies. There are 11 weeklies in Arabic and 3 in French, as well as a small weekly that gives a selection of insignificant news items in stilted English. Specialized periodic publications dealing with the economy, tourism, architecture, and similar topics are exceptionally well done and usually in French. Tunisia has sponsored the publication of an impressive collection of glossy volumes depicting the country's heritage, its scenery, and particularly picturesque towns and villages.

NOTES

1. Abdelbaki Hermassi, minister of culture, in conversation with the author.
2. Official biography.
3. Sadok Chaabane, *Ben Ali et la Voie Pluraliste en Tunisie* (Tunis: Ceres Editions, 1996), p. 89.
4. Ibid.
5. *Human Rights in Tunisia: Choices and Achievements* (Tunisian government publication, 1997), pp. 8–9.
6. Official text.
7 Abdelaziz Ben Dhia in conversation with the author.
8. Ibid.
9. Ibid.
10. Mohamed Harmel in conversation with the author.
11. Ibid.
12. Chaabane, *Ben Ali et la Voie Pluraliste*, p. 108.
13. Ibid., p. 109.
14. Michael C. Dunn, *Renaissance or Radicalism? Political Islam: The Case of Tunisia's al-Nahda* (Washington, D.C.: International Estimate, 1992), p. 48.
15. Chaabane, *Ben Ali et la Voie Pluraliste*, p. 127.
16. Mustapha Khammari, director, the Dar Asssabah company, in conversation with the author.
17. Mohamed Belhadj Amor in a written statement for the author.
18. Official U.S. Congress text.
19. Oussama Romdhani in conversation with the author.
20. Official text of the speech.
21. Author's translation of the answers from the French.
22. Ben Ali's statement to the author.
23. *Afrique Magazine*, December 1989.
24. Official text of the 10th anniversary speech.
25. Ibid.

CHAPTER 7

Friendship in All Directions

Circumventing often contradictory regional tendencies, placating neighbors who are not always convenient or accommodating, and coping with the sequels of the colonial era, Tunisia has managed something that has eluded most countries: friendship in all directions. Despite early, and inevitable, disagreements with France, tiffs with its Arab brothers caused by Bourguiba's bluntness, or events beyond its control, Tunisia's foreign policy has managed to overcome the difficulties of an era rife with conflict. Tunisia has no territorial claims or border disputes. Its diplomacy reaches as far as Tokyo and Buenos Aires. Being Arab, African, and Mediterranean, it has succeeded in blending its colorful past and its modern-age ambitions in an exceptionally successful package.

"Selling" Tunisia to the outside world, particularly during the Ben Ali presidency, has not been difficult, but it has required a constant and sustained diplomatic effort. An example has been set by the president himself, who has traveled to distant capitals and has hosted many foreign visitors. Both are time-consuming and often costly. The main dividend is that not only is Tunisia a country without enemies, but it has friends across the globe.

Such a far-reaching and wide-ranging approach to diplomacy by a small country has helped trade and tourism and has allowed Tunisia to envisage a higher standard of living in the foreseeable future. The ambition of becoming a "young developed nation" at the beginning of the next millennium has been unquestionably helped by Tunisia's diplomatic efforts.

Tunisia's objectives and the need for the good will of the outside world have been constantly stressed by Ben Ali to his diplomats. For example, addressing Tunisian ambassadors and heads of diplomatic missions around the world in August 1995, he said,

It is imperative that our diplomats be thoroughly aware of the importance of their roles in the task of development, so that they will increase their preparedness for any event and keep abreast of changes, with the help of continued promotion of their function, their powers and their programs, and constant protection of their country's interests in every domain. For it is the diplomat's responsibility to strengthen his country's prestige, consolidate its position among the nations of the world, highlight its accomplishments and gains, and make known the contributions it has made to realizing universal aspirations of peace, security and progress.[1]

Ben Ali's idea was to form a new generation of "diplomat-salesmen," whose job would combine official representation with efforts to pave the way to new partnership projects, at the same time publicizing the country's image. It was with that concept in mind that a "diplomatic academy" was opened in Tunis in 1997.

His own diplomatic efforts range far and wide: during the two years preceding completion of this study, he traveled to Japan, Argentina, Germany, Italy, and France. He hosted Pope John Paul in a gesture to underline his campaign for "a climate of tolerance." At international conferences he urged a consensus on how to fight extremism and terrorism.

As pointed out earlier, the sailing has not always been smooth. What has since been labeled Tunisia's middle-of-the-road diplomacy required time and adjustment after a long period of colonial rule. The Tunisians like to say they have combined their three millennia of experience and geographical advantage, being located in the middle of cross-currents sweeping Black Africa, the Middle East, and southern Europe. While unquestionably daunting, such a combination has also induced and inspired ambitious diplomacy, something Ben Ali has sought from the beginning of his regime.

To quote Ben Ali's statement to his diplomats again, "the revolution in communications and information we are experiencing today requires that we rationalize cooperation and coordination of diplomacy, communication, and information, for these are sectors that complement one another in presenting and publicizing our country's accomplishments in all fields."[2]

At the beginning of its modern-age independence in 1956, Tunisia's relations with France were, inevitably, complicated by the war in neighboring Algeria. Since the union of the Maghreb countries is part of Tunisia's constitution, there was no choice. Tunisia could not refuse (even had it wanted to) granting bases and other forms of succor to the FLN, although at times its own population had to suffer from reprisal raids and other forms of economic and political pressure. The idea of a united Maghreb was the linchpin of Tunisia's early foreign policy, although, in retrospect, the results are meager. Still, Tunisia had to live up to its constitution and maintain its "Arab credentials."

Some Tunisians explain this policy not by "historical nostalgia," but by "political necessity and economic pragmatism."[3] Yet to this day, despite the initial plan of Maghreb unity adopted at the 1958 conference in Tangier, each of the Maghreb countries has a different economic and political system and trades with the European "North" rather than with each other or the African "South." Those who doubt in the future of a regional union claim that a "policy of blocs" implies more problems than advantages for a country such as Tunisia. The doubts were intensified in recent years when, despite formal pledges of Maghreb unity, Tunisia—as well as the other members of the potential union—have been individually stressing the advantages of links with the European Union rather than of a vague North African pact with limited economic benefits.

From the beginning of Tunisia's independence, while being consistently in favor of friendly and even warm relations with the United States, Bourguiba pursued a diplomacy of openness toward the communist countries. Although Tunisia established diplomatic relations with the Soviet Bloc countries during the first post-independence years, their activity was limited. There was a small Soviet loan to help finance a dam and a technical school. There have been limited economic ventures by Poland, Czechoslovakia, and several others.

Initially, Bourguiba shunned recognizing China, presumably feeling that his good working relationships with Washington and his rather uneasy friendship with France might be jeopardized by early recognition of Peking. "But when he discovered that de Gaulle was planning recognition in January 1964, the American objections that were probably passed on to him discreetly did not change his decision to beat de Gaulle to the punch if possible, even if only by a few days."[4] Bourguiba appears also to have been prodded by some editorialists who wrote that it was ridiculous to ignore China and keep it outside the international community.

Thus, when the then Chinese prime minister, Chou En-lai, embarked on his first visit to Africa in December 1963, a stopover in Tunis was quickly arranged. Chou and his party arrived in Tunis for two days on January 9, 1964, and, after a reception in the presidential palace, they in turn, invited Bourguiba to a dinner open to the press in the Majestic Hotel. As was his habit, Bourguiba mixed humor with some significant political warnings. He particularly objected to the contrast between the Chinese visitor's theme of "peaceful coexistence" and his perpetual attacks on the United States. In the end, Chou left Tunisia with recognition in his pocket. It took four months for the first Chinese envoy to arrive in Tunis, but when China asked for the accreditation for a staff of 250, the Tunisians reduced it to 40. China, in the throes of its diplomatic and economic offensive in Africa, thought that Tunisia was "a reasonably well-organized one-party state" and "one of the soundest and most stable countries in all Africa"[5] and would have been an ideal springboard for the continent's penetration. Bourguiba quickly signaled the limits of this new relationship, demonstrating that Tunisia was no dupe to foreign designs.

On February 17, 1989, a little over a year after replacing Bourguiba, Ben Ali signed a document on the "creation of the union of Arab Maghreb" at a conference held in Marrakech. The treaty commits all five participants— Tunisia, Libya, Algeria, Morocco, and Mauritania—to the principle of the construction of regional unity, to a common policy in different fields, while remaining vague on many other subjects. Thus, in the field of common defense, the charter merely pledges "to preserve the independence of each member country," and as far as economy is concerned, it calls for member states to "foster industrial, agricultural, commercial and social development."[6] Such obvious objectives seemed hardly worth a major conference, especially since there has been little concrete follow up, besides special immigration desks for the "citizens of the Arab Maghreb" at airports across North Africa, a secretariat and a system of periodic summits and other meetings.

As late as the middle of 1997, Ben Ali appears to have taken the construction of the Maghreb seriously, even though it included such seemingly incompatible states as Gadhafi's "revolutionary" Libya, Tunisia with its presidential democracy, Algeria in the throes of Islamic terror, the Moroccan monarchy, and Mauritania on the fringes of all international activity, a forgotten desert state in a technicolor setting. In fact, from the outset of the Change, Ben Ali kept repeating his conviction that "Tunisia will spare no effort to move the idea of Maghreb unity to the phase of its effective realisation."[7] The following year, on December 8, he stressed that "for us, the idea of Arab Maghreb without frontiers is not a Utopian theory or an unattainable dream." In New York on November 13, 1989, again he repeated that "the Union of Arab Maghreb is a project which fulfills the aspirations of successive generations of the people of the Maghreb and which fits into the pattern of the present day changes marked by the emergence of regional groupings."

During the next few years, a stunned world watched as the Soviet Union disintegrated into bigger and smaller fragments and Yugoslavia exploded into ethnic states, each demanding its independence and its own specific system. On January 14, 1993, the Tunisian president, upon assuming the rotating chairmanship of the Union of Arab Maghreb, preferred to speak of the emerging European unity as an example for the Maghreb. "We are determined to double our efforts and to work steadfastly, with the agreement of our brothers to strengthen relations between our Union and the European Community, and, above all, the European countries bordering on the western Mediterranean."[8]

Solidifying Tunisia's own "Mediterranean vocation," rooted in three millennia of its history, was the signing, on July 17, 1995, of an association agreement with the European Union (EU). In addition to being an unprecedented step for a North African country, for Tunisia it was a portent of a better future—anchored in Europe. The European Union formally acknowledged Tunisia's eligibility to such a partnership, and, consequently, recognized the validity of its system as that of a democratic state. According to the EU communique, economically this was due to the "important progress of Tunisia and of the Tunisian people toward the objective of full integration of the Tunisian economy into the global economy." The political significance in the agreement was a reminder that the new partners "attach particular importance to the respect of the United Nations Charter and, particularly, to the respect of human rights and of the political and economic freedom which constitute the very basis of the association." For Ben Ali, so often crticized in Amnesty International reports, it was a major triumph.

It became clear, over the years, that Tunisian foreign policy attached more importance than its sister states to the concept of Maghreb unity. Repeated calls by the Tunisian president for a joint awareness of the area's problems seem to have fallen not so much on deaf ears as on countries too preoccupied by struggle with their internal problems, which in effect prevented any concrete step toward unity. Thus in mid-1997, Libya remained an international pariah with the continued United Nations ban on its air links, the problem of Western Sahara and the Polissario movement was no nearer solution, and Algeria was sinking deeper into ruthless fratricidal terror. The Maghreb Union was hardly in a position to speak with one voice to the European Union or treat its problems jointly. Unlike Bourguiba who frequently aired in public his various differences with such leaders as Egypt's Gamal Abdel Nasser or Libya's Gadhafi, Ben Ali preferred discreet silence and quiet diplomacy. He was equally tactful toward Tunisia's neighbors, refraining from public comment on their problems and attitudes, although sometimes such comments were extremely tempting.

Two events marked Tunisia's relations with the Arab world: the transfer of the seat of the Arab League from Cairo to Tunis in 1979, and the establishment of the Palestine Liberation Organization (PLO) in Tunis in 1982, following the Israeli invasion of Lebanon and the ouster of the forces of Yasser Arafat from Beirut. In both cases Tunisia acted out of solidarity with its Arab brethren, at the same time reaffirming its allegiance to the Arab community.

The League's departure from Cairo was prompted by Egypt's peace treaty with Israel. The Arabs were not ready to recognize or even digest such a dramatic move by the late Egyptian president Anwar Sadat, and the League's headquarters could not have remained in Sadat's capital, given the level of Arab passions at that time. It had taken 13 years for the Arab world to acknowledge the demands of "realpolitik" in the Middle East, during which time the League's current affairs were ably handled by its new secretary general, Chedli Klibi, a Tunisian Islamic scholar, former information and culture minister and Bourguiba's chief of cabinet. Tunis, previously considered a sleepy city on the fringes of the Arab heartland, had become the capital of the Arab world.

The decision of the League's 20 members to move to Tunis had significant diplomatic implications on the Arab scene. While in Cairo, the League was unquestionably under Egyptian influence. Some claimed it was frequently a tool of Egypt's foreign policy. Indicative of the feelings, at least in some Third World circles, was a statement in *Le Nouvel Afrique Asie* that "for the first time in its existence, the pan-Arab organization, born in Alexandria almost at the same time as the United Nations, stopped being a mere bureaucratic annex of the Egyptian Foreign Ministry to become a true instrument in the service of all Arab states."[9] Tunisia's geographic location, its communications infrastructure, and proximity to the center of European decision-making, were a considerable advantage. Further enhancing Tunisia's role was the fact that it had not been involved in any Arab or Maghreb conflicts.

Klibi's task was extremely difficult. Arab solidarity was quasi-inexistent, and Middle Eastern capitals were opposed to any of the practical reforms suggested by "the Tunisian." In short, and in the face of such dramatic events as the Israeli march on Beirut, the League was paralyzed. Klibi's hands were tied, and his time was consumed by endless negotiations to satisfy the sensitivities of various member states. In the end, when the League decided to give its blessing—including participation of some member states—to an international coalition to oust Saddam Hussein from Iraq, Klibi felt he had no choice but to resign.

The issue was exceptionally delicate and its significance surpassed the context of Tunisia and its diplomacy. Klibi, a quintessential Arab intellectual, felt he had no right to subscribe to military action against one of the League's members (Iraq). He firmly believed in a negotiated solution through Arab efforts, although, in retrospect, such a possibility was a mirage. Still, "the Tunisian" stuck to his principles. He retired to his residence in Carthage, to lecturing and writing. He still feels that any joint Arab action in the Gulf should have been carried out by the Arabs themselves and not under foreign hegemony, as, obviously, was the case during the 1990–1991 Gulf crisis.

Whether or not Tunisia acted correctly in disassociating itself from Desert Storm was debated years later. Ben Ali must have felt like Klibi, but, nonetheless, by sticking to his principles he isolated Tunisia from most Arab countries. Even Syria, a country listed by the U.S. State Department as aiding and abetting international terrorism, sent a contingent to the desert. Those who shared Klibi's strong views felt that Desert Storm was not a war "to liberate Kuwait" but was one to defend the Gulf oilfields. They were probably right, and given the ambitions of the Iraqi strongman, the oilfields, as well as the Strait of Hormuz, had to be secured. The world's industrial powers had to have access to Middle Eastern oil reserves, while oil producers needed a secure and continuing income. Saddam's invasion of Kuwait, carried out in a ruthless manner, precluded all other solutions.

The Muslim countries that participated in the coalition—and they ranged from Morocco to Bangladesh—learned a useful lesson in desert warfare and gained the gratitude of Washington, the primary organizer and leader of the expedition. Jordan, Tunisia, and Algeria, which chose not to take part, needed years of careful diplomacy to explain their motives to an angry State Department. Jordan's attitude was easily justified by its proximity to Iraq and the pro-Iraqi feelings of its large Palestinian population. Years after the crisis, many decisionmakers in Washington still did not understand Ben Ali's attitude. Some thought (and still do) that Ben Ali had backed "the wrong horse," and that he had underestimated Washington's determination to contain Saddam Hussein. There was a theory in Foggy Bottom that Ben Ali was too preoccupied with his domestic Islamists and did not want to risk their wrath. Yet the Arab country most involved in the conflict was Saudi Arabia, the site and guardian of some of Islam's holiest places.

Desert Shield, subsequently Desert Storm, did not foster Western or other colonial interests in the Arab world. It succeeded in keeping Arab wealth in Arab hands, allowing the continuing flow of Western cash into Arab coffers. It required several trips to Washington by Ben Ali's able foreign minister, Habib Ben Yahia, to assuage the hurt feelings of the United States. In the end, diplomacy prevailed. But Tunisia's attitude during that conflict is likely to be remembered in Washington for some time to come.

Following the hesitant behavior during the 1990–1991 Gulf crisis, Ben Ali moved to shore up relations with the Gulf countries, at the same time seeking to make Tunisia's voice heard at various Arab conferences. The improved relations with the Gulf included visits to Tunisia by the Kuwaiti and Qatari leaders and, in 1997, by Prince Bandar Ibn Sultan Ibn Abdelaziz, brother of King Fahd and Saudi ambassador to the United States. (The prince arrived in a large official plane, accompanied by aides and eight body guards. Before he checked into his suite at the brand new Palace Hotel in seaside Gammarth outside Tunis, police using sniffing dogs conducted a minute search for explosives.)

It was hard to assess whether such good will visits went beyond normal diplomatic politeness or whether Tunisia was really exploring other possibilities and dimensions in its relations with its Arab brethren. Ben Ali's aides liked to say that the president was more in tune with the Arab world than was Bourguiba," whose attitude was marked by various ups and downs and unexpected verbal outbursts. Ben Ali carefully avoided controversy and, at Arab summits, urged a "policy of consensus," rarely an easy task in that part of the world.

In August 1982, after an Israeli blitz against its bases in southern Lebanon, the flight of more refugees, and a long and bloody siege of Beirut, the PLO and its leader, Yasser Arafat, were forced to leave the Lebanese capital. They left, firing their guns into the air and pledging, as they so often had, "no, no to kneeling, and yes, yes to fighting."[10] A handful of Arab countries offered to shelter the dispirited and yet undaunted Palestinian fighters, and the largest contingent headed for Tunis. Above all, Tunisia offered its hospitality to Arafat and the PLO leadership, thus becoming a center of Palestinian politics, foreign policy, and military planning for 12 years. Once again Tunisia proved its Arab vocation, disregarding possibly dangerous repercussions. Thus a number of innocent Tunisians were killed during an Israeli reprisal air raid on Hammam Chott near Tunis on October 1, 1985. The raid reminded the Tunisians of the French attack on Sakiet Sidi Youssef in 1958. Again, hospitality to its Arab brethren turned out to be costly to Tunisia.

In addition to the air raid, the Israelis further demonstrated an intricate knowledge of the Palestinian deployment in Tunisia by sending a seaborne commando that killed Abu Jihad, the PLO's military commander, in his suburban villa. The killings added to Tunisia's insecurity and thus increased its burden.

While most Palestinian fighters, initially kept in camps far from the capital, eventually left Tunisia to be closer to the areas of confrontation with the Jewish state, the leadership remained. For 12 years, Tunisian police and security services were deployed around several dozen villas in the suburb of Belvedere and in seaside La Marsa and Gammarth, protecting PLO officials and Arafat, who liked to change his quarters, frequently more than once a day, for security reasons. A stream of foreign journalists regularly visited Tunis in search of Palestinian news—as did Israeli agents under all sorts of cover. Already battling the rising Islamic threat, Tunisia had to cope with yet another problem.

The exposure to Israeli reprisals did not deter Tunisia from seeking to serve as a bridge that would bring Israel and the Palestinians together. Contacts facilitated by Tunisia led to the 1992 "Oslo Agreement" which paved the way to a formal treaty between the Jewish state and the PLO. A Tunisian diplomat, Abdelay Sghaier, thus summed up how he perceived his country's role:

Tunisia served as the site of the first U.S.–PLO dialogue and continued as a conduit for messages between Palestinians and Israelis before and after the Madrid conference that opened the formal Palestinian-Israeli peace process, and the Oslo accords that turned the results of those talks into a formal Israeli–Palestinian treaty.[11]

Voicing Tunisia's dismay at the obstacles that threatened to scuttle the peace process in 1996 and 1997, blamed by Arab states on the hawkish government of Prime Minister Benjamin Netanyahu, Sghaier said, "How can we achieve progress in the economic field if there is no progress in the peace process? The economic dimension is designed to reflect progress in the political field. One cannot put the cart before the horse."[12]

Yet, before the peace talks began to founder, Tunisia was optimistic and sought to go beyond the establishment of token diplomatic missions with the Jewish state. In October 1994, as the process of rapprochement between the Arabs and Israel seemed to be gathering momentum, Foreign Minister Habib Ben Yahia outlined a plan under which Tunisia would seek joint business ventures with Israel. He made his proposal while in Washington for talks on how to advance the peace process, in order to "finish the unfinished symphony."[13] At the time, Tunisia was planning to send a team of leading businessmen first to the Palestinian territories of Gaza and Jericho, then to Israel.

"We hope such gestures will give a sense of security to the Israelis, showing that Arab countries, and particularly Tunisia, mean business," Ben Yahia said. "We are now in a new phase of Arab–Israeli relations. We know it is not risk-free, but we also know we're making history." Unfortunately, the unfavorable development of Arab–Israeli relations during the subsequent two years paralyzed such imaginative initiatives.

Even after the agreement on Palestinian autonomy, the PLO took some time to leave Tunisian soil, citing a variety of reasons, including the limitations of conducting its world-wide diplomacy from the confines of the Gaza Strip and Jericho. Late in June 1994, Arafat informed his Tunisian hosts that the PLO would keep 32 buildings in Tunis and the vicinity.[14] Among the offices that remained for several months were the Political Department, the Department of National and International Relations, and the Department of Refugee Affairs.

Nine days earlier, Arafat used the Organization of African Unity (OAU) summit, held in Tunis, to bid an emotional farewell to his host country and to Africa. "Our Palestinian people are entering a new phase," Arafat told the 42 African heads of state and government gathered in the Tunisian capital. He praised African countries for backing the PLO "on all levels and in all fora, providing it with all kinds of support and assistance."[15]

In the end, the Palestinians left Tunisia—just as the Arab League had returned to Cairo. Tunisia had fulfilled its Arab obligations and was left alone with its highly principled diplomacy and a clear conscience.

As a founding member of the OAU, Tunisia participated in all its summit meetings and ministerial conferences, contributing traditional caution to the often acerbic and passionate debate that characterized that vast regional grouping. To Tunisians, it was clear from the initial summit in Addis Ababa in 1963 that the continent had a long way to go before the term "unity" became significant or practicable. The magnificent reception by Ethiopian Emperor Haile Selassie, the lions chained to the Menelik Palace, the fireworks knifing across the African skies, merely camouflaged a lack of concensus and the stormy reality of the continent of which Tunisia was a part.

At the Tunis OAU summit, Ben Ali called on his guests to demonstrate "more rigor" in coping with problems. "Africa is capable of occupying a central place on the international scene if it applies its skills," he said, speaking as the new chairman of the organization. What Ben Ali had hoped for at the summit was some sort of blueprint for a "new African order" that would make Africa abandon dictatorships and one-party rule and stop treating human rights as a mere slogan.[16] In short, he wanted to create what his aides described as "African awareness of African problems." Subsequently, various participants described the meeting as "the summit of truth," during which neither Ben Ali nor South African President Nelson Mandela neither minced words nor spared their colleagues' sensitivities. Ben Ali himself remarked that the summit was a "decisive turning point in the OAU's history," at which many African statesmen "faced the difficult equation between stability and development."

Three years after the summit, many Tunisian officials felt that the continuing turmoil in sub-Sahara Africa was driving a wedge across the continent, pushing away the Arab nations of the Maghreb after years of struggle for unity. Africa in 1997 was "incapable of speaking with one voice or of exercising any form of international pressure—now or even in the distant future."[17]

The best hope in Tunis was the strengthening of Maghreb unity, a task that Ben Ali and his advisers considered feasible despite the inevitable difficulties. In fact, Maghreb unity appeared to be one of the main targets of Tunisian diplomacy for the new millennium, together with solidifying the "Mediterranean option" with its promise of economic advantages.

NOTES

1. Official Tunisian government text.
2. Ibid.
3. Several officials in conversation with the author.
4. John K. Cooley, *East Wind Over Africa: Red China's African Offensive* (New York: Walker and Company, 1965, p. 175.
6. Author's translation of the official French-language text.
7. Ben Ali's speech in Carthage, December 7, 1987.
8. Author's translation of the official text.
9. *Nouvel Afrique Asia,* June 1996.
10. Arafat on the PLO's departure from Beirut.
11. Abdelhay Sghaier, director of Arab World Affairs in the Tunisian Foreign Ministry, as quoted in *The Washington Report on Middle East Affairs* (November-December 1996), p. 74.
12. Ibid., p. 89.
13. Habib Ben Yahia in an interview in *The Washington Times*, October 7, 1994.
14. Author's dispatch to *The Washington Times*, 22 June 1994.
15. Ibid., 17 June 1994.
16. Ibid.
17. Author's dispatch to *The Washington Times*, 28 April 1997.

CHAPTER 8

Up to the Level

In the morning of April 3, 1997, Kamel Hadj Sassi drove to the village of Regbah about 60 miles southwest of Tunis. The morning was chilly but bright, and spring greenery lay like plush on the surrounding hills. Shepherds wrapped in brown burnouses tended sheep near the winding dirt road cut in the red soil. A bare-legged woman in a bright kerchief led a donkey laden with plastic canisters across the fields, toward a range of mountains towering to the west on the horizon. A normal spring day in Regbah, which will probably not be marked anywhere except in Sassi's appointment diary and in the accounts of his National Solidarity Fund.

Regbah is not on any international maps, but it is very much on the map of the Fund headed by Sassi, which spent exactly $167,000 to eliminate the "zone of darkness" of Regbah. In plain language this meant that the village of 118 households now has a road, electricity, and access to the outside world. It has stopped being a dark spot on Sassi's chart. It was another success for what Tunisians call "26–26."

The magic figure is the number of a special bank account into which the government, institutions, and private companies deposit money as part of the effort to bring light to Tunisia's "shadow areas"—*les zones d'ombre*. The $30 million a year project has helped some 80,000 impoverished families. Since its creation after Ben Ali's takeover, by spring of 1997 it has reduced the "zones of darkness" from 1500 to about 600.

In 1984, 8 percent of all Tunisians lived in *gourbis*, small structures of brick and mud, often covered by thatched roofs. Now only 3 percent live in such homes, replaced by more solid and airy houses with electricity and often with running water.

The watchword of all those involved in Tunisia's struggle against poverty and backwardness is "there is no freedom without development—and no development without freedom."[1] The government has linked the two concepts as schools and infirmaries are built in the former areas of darkness.

Just as Tunisia's efforts on the international scene are often described as middle-of-the-road diplomacy, its economy is said to be a "balancing act." In both cases, Tunisia has claimed success. To wit: during the first 40 years of independence, Tunisia's per capita income in real terms rose fivefold, placing the average Tunisian on a level with a Turk, Pole, or Russian. In 1956, there was one medical doctor for every 5,600 inhabitants, but in 1996 one for 1,500. Life expectancy for men grew from 54 years to 71 years. While at independence only 15 percent of Tunisian households had electricity, in 1996 the figure was almost 90 percent. Similar growth was registered in other fields: in savings accounts, exports, imports, and the state budget. The urban Tunisian has become a major consumer, and 80 percent are home owners. To Tunisian economic planners, the country is no longer "a junior" but has passed onto a higher level of development. It is now "facing the big players in a competition in which the stakes are how to avoid being excluded."[2]

The economic achievements of a country devoid of significant mineral wealth were carried out despite earlier experiments with socialism, and particularly with the system of cooperatives instituted by Bourguiba's former minister of economy, Ahmed Ben Salah. The early difficulties were also compounded by the massive departure of French and Italian settlers and of Tunisian Jews, many of whom held key positions in commerce and in the country's fledgling industries. Thus, as mentioned earlier, the state had to take charge of the economic structure and conduct its development. There was a lot of populism and slogans, vacillation and false hopes. Bourguiba was often shown cooperatives that did not perform well and was given inflated production figures. That sort of "Potemkin village" syndrome turned out to be costly but was eventually overcome, particularly after Bourguiba's removal from power.

From the beginning of the Change, Ben Ali "took position in favor of liberal economy without hesitation or ambiguity."[3] The economic guidelines outlined by the new head of state stressed the necessity of opening to the outside world, liberalizing initiative and creativity in the private sector, and consolidating Tunisia's development potential. Radical reforms were promptly adopted in order to help facilitate imports, investments, reductions of tariffs, and the reinforcement of the local money market. Within six years, Tunisia became a favored state of the International Monetary Fund (IMF), the World Bank, and other international lending organizations. It serviced its debts promptly; it has kept inflation down to 4.8 percent and the budgetary deficit to 1.9 percent of the Gross Domestic Product (GDP). At the same time, private investment in the industrial sector rose to 63 percent and in tourism, Tunisia's leading source of foreign currency, 98 percent.

Tunisia has always been attractive to foreign investors, mainly because of its proximity to Europe and its relatively cheap labor. However, the period of economic and political uncertainty, especially during Bourguiba's last years in office, as well as a number of restrictive measures, kept any influx of foreign capital down. Initially, the so-called offshore companies were not allowed to sell their products on the local market. This measure was alleviated in December 1996, by allowing them to market 20 percent of their production in Tunisia. It was a major opening on the path to the liberalization of trade as Tunisia began preparations to implement its treaty of association with the European Union, an event awaited with enormous hope as well as with trepidation.

There was a great deal of self-satisfaction on the part of government officials in mid-1997, although business circles urged caution, mainly because of the daunting challenge for a country faced with stiff and ruthless competition. Globalization of the economy loomed big on the horizon, and Tunisians were perfectly aware of its challenges, as well as of its inevitable pitfalls. In November 1996, Tunisia hosted a conference on "The Globalization of the Economy and the Countries of the Mediterranean," at which a warning was sounded that economic reforms affecting Europe in the post-communist era could very well threaten the poorer Mediterranean countries. Speakers from both sides of the Mediterranean stressed that before things improved, the gap between the sea's northern and southern shores might first be widened.

Addressing the conference, Ben Ali described globalization as a form of "revolution that has turned the world into a small village." While acknowledging that globalization "is strengthening the foundations of stability and creating effective regional groups," the Tunisian president called for "the creation of Mediterranean awareness in young generations."

"Globalization does not mean assimilation," he said, "just as specificity does not mean isolation or withdrawal. Cultural specifity is a fact which we believe in, and which we make use of for the benefit of humanity and for the promotion of a common struggle for excellence, contribution and variation."[4] He also underlined that "the Mediterranean can have no future without being open to other regions and groups."

The Tunisian press and the media specializing in Third World affairs continued highlighting Tunisia as an example to follow, and with reason. Given the paucity of means, the existence of a firmly embedded bureaucracy, and the limitations of the labor market, Tunisia's performance appears to be almost miraculous. For example, citing a report by the Inter Arab Investment Guarantee Corporation of Kuwait in December 1996, the Tunis

French language daily *La Presse* headlined "Poverty increases in the Arab World but decreases in Tunisia." Indeed, the report claimed that between 1985 and 1990 poverty increased 1.87 percent a year across the Arab world, except in Tunisia, where it decreased 2.2 percent a year.

The Tunisians were quick to stress their progress in the face of considerable difficulties. In advertising copy, Tunisia has become "the little big country," "the country that works," "sixty miles from Europe—an oasis of peace and tranquility." All that has been true since the founder of modern Tunisia was removed from his Carthage palace, making room for a more daring and innovative economic and political policy. To the specialized press, Tunisia has shown that a small Third World country can "make it"—if it applies itself. According to a survey in the *Financial Times* in June 1993, "as a result of its policy of structural adjustment, Tunisia has become a favorite of the International Monetary Fund. It is also a pilot country for certain United Nations social programs."[5] The prestigious British newspaper stressed that although "a course of near-Europeanization is firmly plotted" in Tunisia, it expressed concern for Tunisia's neighbors: "if only the same held next door to the west, where Tunisians are profoundly disconcerted by the threat of incipient guerrilla war in Algeria, or to the east, where Libya continued to ply its own unpredictable, pariah's path!" Four years later, while Tunisia's situation continued improving, that of its neighbors had become even more dramatic.

Analyzing the progress during the first nine years of Ben Ali's regime, the monthly *Global Networks* wrote,

In a volatile region, where the political crisis in neighboring Algeria remains acute and Libya is isolated from the West, Tunisia has sought to maintain stability by implementing tight security and giving as many Tunisians as possible a stake in the fast-growing economy. Ben Ali has made developing regions long-ignored by ex-president Bourguiba a priority.[6]

Some economists tend to divide the post-independence Tunisian economy into four cycles. The first period was that of the country's liberation from the ties binding it to France, the former colonial power. It was a period of experiments and mistakes. Then came Ben Salah's effort to turn Tunisia into a state of quasi-socialist cooperatives, eventually rejected as yet another mistake. In the 1970s there was a major switch under Prime Minister Hedi Nouira, resulting in liberalism and strong economic growth. These achievements were eventually eroded during Bourguiba's last years in power amidst vacillation and a lack of decision on the highest level.

"The road to economic maturity was neither straightforward nor easy," wrote *Le Nouvel Afrique Asie*.

But the lesson drawn from the experience of the first "liberal" attempt between 1956–1961, until the "wild liberalism" of the 1970s, and through eight years of "specific socialism," permitted the forging of a new approach. Since 1987, it has been characterized by social market economy, such as exists in many European countries. While allowing enterprises to create wealth, this approach delegates to the state the role of a regulator, which is indispensable to national cohesion and for the defense of national interests.[7]

Although possessing a class of low- and middle-level bureaucrats trained under the colonial administration, Tunisia was not adequately prepared to face independence, particularly since its various economic efforts were frequently blocked by the former colonial power, which kept control of the banking system. There was a sudden and unexpected devaluation of the Tunisian dinar in 1959—to the surprise of most government officials—which eventually led to a new economic policy as a new team of technocrats made its uncertain first steps.

It took three decades before Tunisia became *l'enfant cheri* of the IMF, and before the U.N. Development Program listed it as being 85th among the world's nations according to the "human development index," a composite based on economic achievements as related to general well-being. Tunisia, according to that report for 1994, "in the first place used its resources to improve the standard of living, assuring an equilibrium between the demands of development and those of a social nature." In 1995, Tunisia's position moved up to 75th. As far as the degree of equality between the sexes was concerned, Tunisia rated 59th among the 130 countries surveyed by the U.N. organization.

When Tunisia marked the 40th anniversary of its independence in 1996, some analysts described it as having matured "into the most stable economy in North Africa," in an area "where anxiety so often outweighs confidence."[8]

The delicate balancing act of opening up a formerly state-dominated economy to market forces without jeopardizing the living conditions of major sectors of the population has been achieved while keeping the budget under control. Debt problems, which emerged a decade ago, have been mastered without re-scheduling. Current account convertibility was introduced in 1994 and full convertibility is a realistic target for the coming years.[9]

In the months that followed, some stock market analysts claimed that Tunisia's reforms could proceed at a faster pace through an accelerated privatization and the wider opening of the Tunis *bourse* (stock exchange) to foreign investors. Some World Bank officials, however, complained that privatization in Tunisia affected mainly small companies, while leaving the bulk in government hands. That was not the case of tourism, the main foreign currency earner, in which, by 1997, 90 percent of hotels were owned by private capital.

Among other complaints in what seemed to be a smooth economic adjustment was that of a heavy bureaucracy permeating all levels of decision making and execution. For example, one World Bank official claimed that "it takes sometimes 15 days to clear a container in Tunis harbor while the same procedure requires only 15 minutes in Singapore." To obtain a simple document from a Tunisian government department in 1997 was still an arduous task.

There is no doubt that the biggest single event in Tunisia's economic history was the July 17, 1995, association agreement with the European Union. The agreement will join Tunisia, in about the year 2010, to the now 15 EU nations—probably more by then—in a free-trade zone of more than 360 million people. It represents an enormous opportunity as well as an enormous challenge. It has forced Tunisia to change its economic thinking and adjust its planning to that of its European partners.

The key phrase of this crucial transition period is *la mise à niveau*— roughly translated as "coming up to the level." In short, Tunisian companies have to modernize and streamline everything, from staff training to equipment, to face competition from Europe. This new and gigantic "window of opportunity" is also fraught with concern. "Tunisia is now engaged in a struggle for survival in a highly competitive world," said Hedi Mechri, director of L'Economiste Maghrebin, an economic journal. "We have accepted the challenge of competition but the economy is yet to be adapted. Still, we have understood the need to think internationally. We no longer have the complex of the colonized."[10]

For the European Union, its agreement with Tunisia was a major step in drawing the economies of the southern Mediterranean countries closer into Europe's orbit. Eventually, a free-trade zone will encompass much of the Arab world, after Tunisia's pioneering experience. Ahead economically of their southern Mediterranean neighbors, Tunisian economists understood that "only by creating the conditions which attract large-scale investment flows could an emerging market in the southern Mediterranean produce sustained growth and higher living standards."[11]

On a number of occasions, Ben Ali underlined the importance of Mediterranean solidarity in future economic planning. "Throughout its history, the Mediterranean has been a unified entity and the cradle of civilizations and revealed [sic] religion," he said in November 1996.

It has thus become a bridge for communication between the countries on its borders, and a fertile soil for the values of tolerance, liberty, and cooperation. Today, it is called upon to contribute to the building of the future of humanity as it has contributed to the building of its past.[12]

While stressing Tunisia's Mediterranean links of the past and expectations in the future, Ben Ali was quick to understand that technical progress and Tunisia's industrial drive can only be helped by an expanded knowledge of English. This awareness was accentuated during his visit to South Africa in 1995, when he saw that very few members of his entourage were fluent in English. What followed was a directive to make English-language classes compulsory in the first two years of university education. The measure was subsequently expanded to secondary schools. It was part of the country's effort in "coming up to the level," the theme dominating the entire business and technical spectrum.

The industrial expansion that started attracting foreign investment began in earnest in 1988 with a structural adjustment program approved by the International Monetary Fund. By 1994, the gross domestic product grew almost 30 percent in real terms. In subsequent years it settled to about 4 percent annually, with industry emerging as the driving force of economic growth. According to a statement in 1995 by Slaheddine Bouguerra, minister of industry,

what is important has been the rate of growth over the past three years. While the economy as a whole has been growing around 4.8 percent, industry has grown by about 7.5 percent over the same period. If you consider that we're expecting GDP to grow 4 percent this year, but the agricultural sector to decline 6 percent and tourism to be flat, then it becomes clear that it is the industrial sector which is pushing the economy.[13]

Tunisian officials stress that during an exceptionally difficult period in the early 1990s marked by a recession in Europe, its main trading partner, and the fallout of the Gulf war with its impact on tourism, "Tunisia never wavered from its commitment to a market oriented economy." An important step was the launching, in 1994, of the first Tunisian international bond issue, a Samurai bond in Japan. Other bond issues followed in several international financial centers.

Of considerable significance was the eager entry on the Tunisian scene of foreign energy companies. Compared to its neighbors, Libya and Algeria, Tunisian energy supplies are limited although some areas, particularly offshore, are still untapped. "There was a time, in the 1970s, when we were producing five times more oil than we consumed. Our production of 100,000 barrels per day is roughly equal to our consumption. Energy used to account for about 20 percent of gross domestic product. Now it contributes only about 6 percent," said Abdelwaheb Kesraoui, director general of energy.[14] What attracts foreign energy prospectors is Tunisia's liberal policy governing exploration. It is a system, at one stage considered to be revolutionary, under which the government's share of profits escalates only on the basis of the rate of recovery of gas or oil.

By far the most important project is the Miskar offshore gas field near Sfax, developed by British Gas Tunisia, which has been operating since May 1995 and supplies at least 30 percent of Tunisia's gas demand.

Considering such favorable factors as structural reforms based to a great extent on political stability, at the end of 1996 Tunisia still had a long way to go to reach European standards. The European Union estimated that should further transition or the process of "moving up to the level" be mishandled, some 2,000 small Tunisian companies could go bankrupt and another 2,000 might be in financial difficulties. The government seems to be aware of the problem and has adopted a policy of bringing 400 companies to a competitive level every year over a period of ten years. The results were yet to be properly assessed when this study was written.

The cost of the first part of the transition between 1996 and 1999 was initially estimated at over $2 billion, of which the bulk (60 percent) was earmarked for developing local companies, and the rest for infrastructure and improvement of what officials describe as " the business environment." The Tunisians hoped for some financial support from the European Union, but it was clear that the bulk of the effort would have to be borne by Tunis and not Brussels.

The costly and basically still uncertain process of the *mise à niveau*, over a period of 12 years was described as follows by the economic publication *Global Networks:*

The "mise à niveau" aimed to bring Tunisian industry up to a level comparable with its European counterparts—which is crucial to the country's economic future. As tariff barriers are dismantled, Tunisian companies will be forced to adapt themselves to a steadily increasing influx of European goods.

To achieve the necessary transformation, local enterprises must revitalize their entire organization before new, more competitive products hit the market. This involves the overhauling of their management and marketing techniques; the skills and salaries of their workforce; training procedures; financial structures; and production equipment. In some cases, firms will have to merge, or substantially increase their capital to launch new products and take on the competition. Consolidation in traditional industries will be essential: the opening of the local market to European products threatens to eliminate around 30 percent of Tunisian industry, with all the negative consequences that that implies for employment.[15]

Despite considerable pitfalls, Tunisia has accepted the challenge. The economy is still in its struggling stage and consists mainly of small- and medium-sized enterprises. The per capita income was estimated in 1996 as $2,900 a year, which some Tunisian officials like to translate as $5,000, considering the low cost of fruit, vegetables, and housing compared to that of European countries. Six percent of the population lives below what is considered poverty level, and 60 percent consider themselves to be middle class.

The biggest threat in "coming up to the level" is to the employment situation. An educated Tunisian with technical skills had no trouble finding work in 1997. Most of the estimated 350,000 unemployed were among manual laborers, unlikely to benefit from the drastic restructuring of the economy. That was especially important as Tunisian policy makers and technocrats insisted that people were the country's main wealth. "We are building upon the only resource we have: the people," said Mohammed Ghannouchi, minister of international cooperation and foreign investments. "At this stage we know where we're going. And we also know we can count only on ourselves."[16]

Because of the continuing stress on people as Tunisia's main asset, the success of the "coming up to the level" largely depends on the country's ability to absorb its unemployed. The best proposed solution, going back to 1993, was that Tunisia needed to create at least 60,000 jobs a year—just to keep unemployment from growing. While the previously threatening birthrate was thought to be generally under control in the mid-1990s, unemployment and under-employment remained a major problem. According to foreign businessmen involved in Tunisia, any sizeable reduction of unemployment could only come from an increased implantation of foreign firms. Despite Tunisia's many attractive features, that was likely to be slow, certainly not on a scale to make a big dent in the number of jobless. On the other hand, the inevitable streamlining and amalgamation of the existing businesses did not bode well for the problem of unemployment, which also remained the key dilemma in such industrial powers as Germany and France as Tunisia entered the minefield of the "coming up to the level."

Consequently, Tunisia's technocrats have to find solutions to the urgent problem of industrial expansion combined with expensive social policies considered to be essential if the country is to have a satisfied labor force. The government's reaction so far has been that "we do not want to break records of competitiveness by sacrificing local standards."[17] Thus a minimum wage has been introduced, at about $100 a month, or one-tenth of that of France. That level was due to rise with inflation estimated at about 4 percent per annum. What Tunisia certainly could not afford was to lose the advantage of its cheap labor vis-à-vis that of the increasingly active countries of Eastern Europe.

Some foreign businessmen argued that a significant improvement of the economy was only possible with a major relaxation of the political scene, which would reduce the dominant role of the Constitutional Democratic Rally. While allowing a token opposition in the parliament, the government was not ready to face the added problem of a partisan free-for-all similar to that which spelled disaster in Algeria. As 1997 drew to a close, Ben Ali announced a plan to increase the opposition's representation in Parliament as well as in city councils.

The idea in government circles was that Tunisia was still in the process of "democratic apprenticeship," and that democracy had to come by stages. The prevailing opinion among the critics of Tunisia's policies was that "you can't have economic liberalism in a restrictive political environment." The government retorted that the political environment is being steadily re-formed in an exceptionally difficult climate affected by currents inde-pendent of Tunisia, such as Islamic fundamentalism and the instability of Algeria. The majority in the business community felt that stability such as offered by Tunisia was a major asset.

In the lively debate on Tunisia's prospects in 1997, the accent was definitely on the economy rather than on the political evolution. Foreign businessmen and potential investors assumed they would have to continue facing an economic scene dominated by directives emanating from the Carthage palace. In all objectivity, the directives so far have been progres-sive and salutary. What seems to be lacking is critical debate in parliament and the press, something the leadership considered to be premature—and possibly destabilizing as long as Algeria was in the throes of Islamic terror.

Reflecting the country's reality, Tunisian intellectuals and technocrats participating in the debate concentrated mainly on the purely economic aspects of the problem. The accent was on the changing economic scene rather than on a possible political evolution, as well as on the ethnic unity of the country that could shelter Tunisia from the shockwaves of foreign turbulence. Thus, writing in *Jeune Afrique*, Baccar Touzani, secretary general of the Franco-Arab Chamber of Commerce, pointed out that while in 1956, the year of Tunisia's independence from French rule, such minerals as phosphates, lead, and iron ore as well as oil, wine, and dates represented 95 percent of Tunisia's exports, their volume and value in 1995 was reduced to a mere 15 percent.[18]

"The real problems lie elsewhere," he wrote,

Tunisia ought to remain an homogeneous nation and the organization of the state should be re-thought from top to bottom in order to be able to answer the exigencies of a new international economic game. Let's look at the nations on both shores of the Mediterranean. What do we see first? The breakup of nations, caused by religious, ethnic, linguistic, or tribal factors.

Could these shocks affecting our neighbors come to us one day? We only have one indigenous language, one religion and ethnical or tribal compositions are of interest only to ethnologists. We are united and that is our difference.

Echoing the government's views, Touzani criticized the concept of de-mocracy as conceived by the Western media, that is of

a uniform which every state should wear. If one state decides to dress differently, it is dictatorship. If Tunisia, given the nature of its neighbors, does not have a regime similar to that of France, it means there is a democratic deficit in Tunisia. No, democracy is not a uniform. It is adapted to the realities of each country. For democracy to progress in Tunisia, it would be essential to have an admini-stration capable of supervising the democratic advance without creating a deficit of security.[19]

Despite some criticism of the Tunisian political system, foreign investors have shown considerable confidence in the future of the country which, particularly during the last decade of the 20th century, became a vast construction site. The degree of construction has been impressive, from schools and apartment blocks to factories and official buildings. With its sprawling suburbs equipped with shopping malls and fast-food cafes, Tunis is virtually a megalopolis. A competitive private bus service has been established at higher prices but also with more comfort. Supermarkets are replacing the traditional small grocers people used to call *djerbien*, after the inhabitants of the island of Djerba. Foreign visitors nostalgic for old Tunisia find the transformation jarring and colorless. Most Tunisians find their modern life considerably easier.

From the financial markets' point of view, since 1993 there has been a considerable expansion of the Tunis stock exchange, known as *La Bourse des Valeurs Mobilières*. Economists attribute the expansion to the diversification of financial products, the growing rhythm of privatization as well as the extension of capital structures by a number of companies. In such a bullish atmosphere, the stock exchange emerged as a channel for public savings to capitalize local firms in search of new sources of financing.

The reticence of some foreign investors concerning Tunisia in the second half of the last decade was due mainly to the uncertainty in neighboring Algeria. While praising the quality of the Tunisian work force and the generally favorable investment climate, foreign businessmen interviewed by specialized publications inevitably mentioned Algeria. Newsletters on investment advice stress the Tunisian government's commitment to a free market trading regime, but admit that a "risk factor" exists because of the unfavorable situation in Algeria. Significantly, many Tunisians interviewed for this study voiced similar concerns.

Some foreign investors also appeared to be concerned by the month-long fasting period of Ramadan, during which Muslims abstain from eating or drinking from dawn to dusk and end the day with a giant feast. Bourguiba, who stubbornly fought all public religious manifestations, shocked Tunisia, in 1961, by sipping orange juice during a televised appearance in the middle of Ramadan. The advent of political Islam has made the leaders of Tunisia much more careful of Islamic feelings. Foreigners generally assume that little work can be done on contracts and other matters of business during that period and shun Tunisia, finding officials uncomfortable and sleepy. This attitude has been changing with growing privatization, but the obstacle of Ramadan remains.

An editorial in *L'Economiste Maghrebin* read,

While world leaders intoned hymns to the glory of globalization, the Arab world was preparing for the holiday of Aid el Fitr marking the end of month-long hybernation—an eternity by the standards of the end of the century." At a time when the planet's gurus brandish the specter of deregulation, confirm new values and re-design the borders of tomorrow's world, the Arabo-Muslim world limits its horizons to the breaking of the fast and sets the pace of its life by nocturnal vigils which rarely agree with the exigencies of the working day.

The price is a heavy one. The productivity does not resist the sluggishness of society, and quality is among its victims. In short, during a whole month the country lives beyond its means and, paradoxally, national companies profit from an excess of consumption.[20]

The key economic sector in which Tunisia excels is that of tourism. With an estimated four million visitors a year, it is the leading earner of foreign currency, bringing about $1 billion a year. It employs directly some 60,000 people and indirectly 200,000 more and, consequently, feeds more than a million Tunisians. Its progress during the first 40 years of independence has been spectacular, and toward the end of the millennium Tunisia was one of the prime destinations in the Mediterranean.

The stability of Tunisian tourism was demonstrated during 1996, a critical year because of changing travel patterns and the high unemployment rate in Western Europe. While countries such as Greece, Cyprus, and Egypt were losing visitors, Tunisia gained 7 percent in tourism income and was looking toward further increases. Seven hotel schools were turning out high quality personnel, praised by professional publications.

What started with two hotels on the island of Djerba and one in the oasis of Tozeur in about 1960 has expanded into an impressive infrastructure comprising 160,000 hotel beds and four international airports handling a steady stream of visitors. In addition to the international flights in and out of the main Tunis-Carthage airport, in 1997 scheduled international flights linked Western Europe with Djerba and Tozeur in the south and Tabarka in the north. Skanes-Monastir airport was growing steadily, and there were occasional flights to and from Sfax, often called the capital of the Tunisian south.

While at first advertising its perfect sandy beaches and mild climate as the main tourist attraction, Tunisia soon diversified and began stressing cultural trips, facilities for international symposiums and business conferences, as well as Sahara tourism and golf courses for affluent senior citizens. The idea was to get away from the "sun, sand, and sex" aspect of tourism and keep the country's hotels reasonably filled throughout the entire year. According to Tourism Minister Slaheddine Maaoui, Tunisian hotels never close and had an occupancy rate of 52 percent in 1996.[21]

By 1997, the expansion of the hotel infrastructure continued but at a slower pace. Thus subsequent plans called for an additional 7,000 beds a year instead of the previous 10,000. From an average trip of 10 days in the 1980s, the following decade saw shorter trips by European tourists averaging 7.2 hotel nights. In addition to high-rise hotels in Tunis, most structures aimed at tourists were low and blended with the scenery. However, there were complaints about cases of careless development, particularly in the south, with the architecture of new hotels frequently out of character with the environment. Maaoui liked to say to visitors that if all hotels were lined along the coast, they would occupy only 74 kilometers of the 1,200 kilometer coastline. To avoid overcrowding, no new "touristic zones" were being created after 1996, he said. In fact, the government has selected six "protected zones" in which touristic infrastructure is banned.

Roman, Greek, and Phoenician sites are a considerable attraction, as well as the well-organized Sahara tourism. Unusually gifted for foreign languages, Tunisian traders and hotel personnel were soon at ease in German and Italian (in addition to French which most speak from childhood), and were learning such languages as Russian, Polish, or Czech. Officials regarded tourism as more than a source of income. "Tunisians like tourists and feel that the growth of tourism reflects Tunisia's popularity. You can say that tourism is for us a barometer," Maaoui stated, adding "we are perfectly aware of the fact that tourism is changing, that many people no longer want to spend hours roasting in the sun. So, we are constantly thinking of new ways of attracting visitors."[22]

NOTES

1. Sadok Chaabane, *Ben Ali et la Voie Pluraliste en Tunisie* (Tunis: Ceres Editions, 1996), p.81.

2. Baccar Touzani, secretary general of the Franco-Arab Chamber of Commerce, in *Jeune Afrique*, 20 March 1996.

3. Chaabane, *Ben Ali et la Voie Pluraliste*, p. 81.

4. Official government text.

5. *Financial Times*, 14 June 1993.

6. *Global Networks*, 25 March 1996.

7. *Le Nouvel Afrique Asie*, June 1996.

8. *Global Networks*, 25 March 1996.

9. Ibid.

10. In conversation with the author.

11. *Global Networks*, 25 March 1996.

12. Official text, 4 November 1996.

13. Slaheddine Bouguerra in *The Wall Street Journal*, 6 November 1995.

14. *The Wall Street Journal*, 6 November 1995.

15. *Global Networks*, 25 March 1996.

16. Mohammed Ghannouchi in conversation with the author.

17. Ibid.

18. *Jeune Afrique*, 20 March 1996.

19. Ibid.

20. *L'Économiste Maghrebin*, 12 January 1997.

21. Slaheddine Maaoui in conversation with the author.

22. Ibid.

CHAPTER 9

Honing a Nation

The computer in the office of the minister of professional training and employment came to life, and data from 35 trade and technical education centers flashed on the screen. Seconds later, the minister had in front of him the exact figures on the demand for skilled jobs in 11 different fields of Tunisia's industrial production. He then switched to the file showing the availability of the talent required.

In the oasis of Tozeur, on the fringes of the Sahara, 31 eighth-grade pupils repeated after their teacher the key phrase of English lesson number 37: "English is the language of communication, business, science and aviation. Many people learn English to have better jobs."

In her office on Bab Benat Boulevard in the heart of Tunis, Faiza Keffi, president of the National Union of Tunisian Women, reviewed the latest statistics on female behavior in her country: 55 percent used contraceptives, 71 percent of births were assisted by qualified medical personnel, 33 percent of medical doctors were women.

It was a typical morning in Tunisia, a state now considering itself mature after 40 years of an independence marked by major milestones, myriad problems, and impressive successes. From a country deprived of almost everything and dominated by a colonial power with its settlers and bureaucrats, Tunisia is now solidifying what officials like to describe as "nation building." The key elements, honed during those first 40 years, are education, employment, equal status for women, and family planning. These objectives have been duly codified and constitute the basis of the country's political, economic, and social ambitions. Some have been fully achieved, but Tunisians themselves admit that a lot remains to be done. Since the 1987 takeover, the government directed by Ben Ali is making sure that work is done better than in the past.

To Tunisia's present-day young, the pre-independence period seems light years away. The smallest and poorest of the Francophone North African countries, for years Tunisia—at least its indigenous population—was treated as a stepchild of France. Tunisian society was dominated by a score of rich merchant families who represented the local aristocracy and its economic power-base. It had a well-trained class of clerks and administrators—responsible to French officials appointed by the protectorate. Almost 80 percent of its population was illiterate, and half lived in primitive dwellings, usually without electricity or running water. A high infant mortality rate completed this depressing picture.

Perhaps the most tangible and lasting impact of colonial rule was knowledge of the French language, that is, among those Tunisians who were lucky enough to have access to education. The post-independence regimes had enough foresight to continue the teaching of French, and, except for a brief period under the premiership of Mohammed Mzali, on a much larger scale. Years after independence, the instruction of some technical subjects at university level is still in French, although in some fields it is being replaced by English (see below). The knowledge of French—impressive among those with higher education—has basically given Tunisians not only a window on the Western world but a foothold into Europe and a better understanding of the European mentality. No longer patronized by the former colonizers, today's Tunisians can now enjoy the beauty and advantages of the French language without "constraints or complex." Considering that the modern-age Tunisian elite has had a Franco-Arabic education, problems of all sorts are usually analyzed in a Cartesian spirit (albeit with some inevitable procrastination). On the whole, the country is a remarkable example of the amalgamation of two distinct cultures, Arabic and French. In this Tunisia has succeeded better than neighboring Algeria, which was under French rule for 130 years. But Algeria seems to have been burdened by the tremendous complex resulting from the double standard of almost everything prevailing during colonial rule, compounded by the seven-year war of independence and Algeria's inability to achieve economic and social success. While in Tunisia the one-party state in many ways facilitated economic progress, in Algeria it seems to have stifled it.

As Tunisia approaches a new millennium, it is clear that the country's mentality has undergone a profound change. According to the French-language weekly *Jeune Afrique*, a "new concept of being Tunisian is in the process of emerging."[1] In 1997, it was perhaps the only country on the African continent where a majority of the population lived better than during the colonial period, the only one which paid its debts promptly, and the only former colony that climbed from abject poverty to quasi-prosperity, or at least to within reach of prosperity. The path has been adequately traced, and only external factors independent of Tunisia's present regime can thwart its success.

Bourguiba, Tunisia's first president, laid the foundations for the future construction. The Ben Ali regime has consolidated and improved Bourguiba's initial program which, however, unfortunately for Tunisia, was marred by hesitation, corruption, and the absence of leadership during the latter years of the founder's "reign." Above all, under Ben Ali's presidency, Tunisia plunged deeply into a vast program of economic and social reforms, bringing it closer to Europe. Because, despite official slogans of African or Arab unity, the average educated Tunisian aspires to be part of Europe and espouses European values. The colonial mentality and complexes have long disappeared. The relationship with the former colonial power is sane and constructive and, in most cases, marked by mutual respect. Both countries are extremely lucky that old demons have disappeared.

It is interesting to note that some American diplomats, professionally involved with Tunisia in recent years, felt that in chosing Europe, Tunis had chosen "the wrong model" or "backed the wrong horse." Those officials pointed out that Europe at the end of the 20th century was not a particularly successful model to emulate. It was expensive, burdened by social debt, and plagued by unemployment and various problems of adjustment to the post-communist era. Such thinking reflects the idea that, to most Americans, the American model was more successful and the only one worth imitating.

The United States has contributed large sums of money to Tunisia's welfare, apparently with no proverbial "strings" attached. Washington appeared content with Tunisia's pro-Western course and generally understood that the country's main interests lay in creating closer bonds with nearby European states rather than with the distant American continent. In fact, Tunisia was an exceptionally successful laboratory for U.S. aid, which was neither squandered nor used to make Tunisia an instrument of Washington's policy. Tunisia would welcome closer economic ties, but the enormous distance basically precludes them. Although the English language, particularly its American version, is making strong inroads, Tunisia's "Francophonie" is likely to dominate for years to come.

By 1996, virtually all U.S. programs that helped put Tunisia on its feet have been scrapped because Washington considers Tunisia as being on the threshold of development and self-sufficiency. Although sharing this view, many Tunisians felt that by halting its aid, the United States acted mistakenly at a critical stage of the country's economic takeoff. Thus, discussing the problem, the minister of international cooperation and investment, Mohammed Ghannouchi, said, "the United States strongly supported Tunisia in the 1960s and 1970s. Unfortunately, aid slowed in the 1980s and now is practically non-existent."[2]

In 1997, the only U.S. aid program operating in Tunisia was that of the Overseas Private Investment Corporation (OPIC), which gives loans to American firms investing overseas. According to Ghannouchi, "the private sector in the United States could play a major role in Tunisia. Reforms of the past two or three years have improved the investment climate. Foreign investors can freely transfer their profits."[3]

According to a survey on Tunisia conducted by *The Washington Report on Middle East Affairs* in the fall of 1996

most of the private U.S. economic interest in Tunisia has been in the energy sector. Leading U.S. participants to date have been Texaco and Marathon petroleum in the oil exploration and drilling field, and Citibank, which has been established in Tunisia for several years and plays a major role in Tunisian banking. In manufacturing, Packard Electric, a subsidiary of General Motors, employs 1,500 workers in the assembly of vehicle harnesses for export to Europe, and Nabisco packages food products for the Middle East in Tunisia.[4]

Justifiably, the new generation of educated Tunisians is satisfied with the economic and social results obtained by its leadership. Many young Tunisians talk about their country as "a pocket of stability in an area of instability." Phrases such as "we haven't exactly been spoiled by our neighbors" are frequently heard. The government, predictably, prefers not to publicize such views, likely to strain its relations with those cumbersome neighbors, both of which envy Tunisia the way it has handled its development.

The Tunisian young who crowd the growing university campuses are relatively distant from politics. One major reason is the general disinterest in political ideologies, and perhaps it is also the result of the destabilizing and disruptive influence of the period of Islamic agitation. According to Rachid Driss, a venerable old diplomat who served Tunisia throughout its most difficult years, "what the average young Tunisian wants is work, health care, prosperity."[5] According to his analysis, there is a keen interest in foreign affairs but considerably less in any reformist ideas, perhaps because the young feel the regime is doing an adequate job. The regime means progress, Driss said, "and in this sense we are unique in the Arab world. The opposition can only offer different personalities rather than different solutions."

Such an analysis is confirmed by various personal and published interviews with Tunisia's young people. All showed a strong "middle class" mentality, awareness of world problems, a desire for higher material gains and basic satisfaction with the government's policies. In the middle of the 20th century's last decade, it was hard to discern any revolutionary tendencies among Tunisia's future elites. Obviously, the government made sure that such tendencies threatening to disrupt the existing order are not encouraged, without making any form of coercion obvious.

It can be said that after 40 years of independence, Tunisia was dominated by its growing middle class, a family of four, often with two salaries, a mortgage on an apartment or house, a car bought on credit, and children at school and aspiring to higher education. Those in the higher income bracket bought satellite dishes and planned trips abroad. Hard-working, though not particularly affluent by Western standards but slowly getting there, this Tunisian middle class constitutes the basis, and in a way it orients the government's economic and social planning. Higher education dominates the family's agenda and political issues seem distant. Such factors played a key role in the regime's success in containing Islamic fundamentalism, reducing its impact, and making it—at this writing—basically irrelevant as a political force.

According to the weekly *Jeune Afrique*, directed by a veteran Tunisian journalist but published in Paris,

culturally, the country has become less homogeneous. Swayed by economic progress and by the opening to the world, the standardized models have been shattered. The rapid increase in the standard of living and of education have created several types of Tunisians. The increasingly growing intellectual and economic elite is Mediterranean oriented, urban, frequently French-speaking, and more and more demanding. It wants to go faster both in the battle of development as well as in the battle for the freedom of expression. This society, once dominated by men, is now wide open to women. At the place of work, the integration of women has become a permanent revolution. Equally revolutionary are relations within the family. The financial independence of women has re-shaped family relations. The young no longer accept moral rules imposed by parents. Thus a new Tunisian synthesis is being created, consisting of often contradictory elements. The new elite wants to be Arab but also cosmopolitan. It is tempted by both freedom and state control.[6]

In the field of primary and secondary education, one milestone is the 1991 educational reform, a multi-faceted set of parameters to guide the young generations into the 21st century. The boldness and innovative nature of some of its facets have astounded a number of observers and have served as an example to other Arab countries.

The reform was prompted by the feeling that the previous system had run out of steam and had to be modernized in keeping with the country's general orientation. Among the essential changes was the adding of such subjects as arts, music, and computer science (the latter still on a limited scale) and the expansion of the teaching of languages. French, the dominant foreign language, is taught from the third year. English is now required in the eighth year. Young Tunisians also have to choose another foreign language among Spanish, Italian, and German. All told, the secondary-level pupils go to classes 28 hours a week, of which six hours are devoted to foreign languages.

The overriding idea, according to Education Minister Hatem Ben Oth-man, is "to develop an aesthetic sense, respect for manual labor and instill the need for an opening on the outside world."[7] The teaching of history was revised to include the essentials of Tunisia's known existence during three millennia, particularly stressing those that have influenced the country's character. Thus, according to a popular slogan, "Hannibal was one of us." In old textbooks, history generally started with the Arab conquests.

Equally affected by the reform was the teaching of Arabic, for years treated as a "dead language"—practically as Latin is in Western schools. The revised program includes contemporary Arab writers and texts stress-ing modern Arabic views and culture while "rejecting anything that is backward and intolerant," according to Ben Othman. The minister particu-larly underlined the opposition of the authorities to any plans for a too assertive "Arabization" that would reduce the impact of the prevailing French approach to education.

An interesting innovation was the "Arabization" in the teaching of science and mathematics, under which texts are in Arabic but figures and symbols of chemical formulae in standard Latin characters. Consequently, students have to acquire the ability of being able to read the text from right to left and the figures in the opposite direction—on the same page. Such a system apparently intrigued several other Arab countries trying to find the best methods of combining Arabic with Western scientific instruction.

The educational reform involved a massive effort in preparing teachers for their new role. This included intensive summer courses as well as famili-arization trips to France, Italy, Canada, and Belgium. The government re-viewed education programs of other Arab countries to "avoid the mistakes of several of our Arab brothers," according to Ben Othman, who was not specific on this subject. Tunisia, he stressed, was determined to "develop its own specific educational system," and felt satisfied that a new generation would be more at ease in Arabic while, at the same time, speak better French than the old one. New Tunisian teachers were described as "adopting many points of view and angles of vision" and rejecting a one-sided approach.

Various educators interviewed by the author insisted that the initiative for such a sweeping and modern approach emanated from Ben Ali himself, the product of military schools rather than of traditional academia. The president, one teacher said, "is a man of his era."

At the end of 1996, Tunisia spent one-third of its budget on education at all levels. Of the 380,000 state employees, 134,000 were teachers. A total of 2.2 million students were enrolled in the educational system. According to some Tunisians, in addition to creating an exceptionally well educated country, such a massive effort was instrumental in defusing the tension and revolutionary tendencies that marked the universities in the 1980s. "At one stage university students tended toward the left, were militant, organizing strikes and demonstrations and discussing utopian ideas of a new society," said Mohamed Harmel, a former communist and subsequently general secretary of the Ettadjid movement, a small opposition party.[8] "The young used to talk about radical causes, including support for Libya and Iraq, the dream of Arab unity. All that has changed. The political involvement of our youth has collapsed."

Perhaps the biggest expansion in the educational system took place at university level. Between 1987 and 1996, the number of students in institutions of higher learning doubled, to exactly 112,624 of whom 43.7 percent were women, at the country's six universities. Dali Jazi, minister of higher education, estimated at the beginning of 1997 that by the year 2007, the number would grow to 275,000, considering the stability of Tunisia's birthrate of 1.8 percent.[9]

The steady growth has been accompanied by a change in programs, favoring sciences and business administration in a country where previously students were overwhelmingly inclined toward humanities. "Graduates in fine arts and literature are simply condemned to unemployment while the others usually get a job within a year of graduation," Jazi said. "Tunisia's development lies in technology." This change was accompanied by an expansion of the compulsory teaching of English, stimulated by Ben Ali.

Because of the expected growth of the student body, the government has made plans to spend $600 million during a period of five years on university infrastructure and training of the educators. Increasingly, candidates for university-level posts are sent for training to the United States, Canada, and Belgium rather than to France. Jazi estimates that at least until the year 2002, Tunisia will need between 650 and 1,000 new university-level instructors a year. At the beginning of 1997, a total of 6,000 students were studying for doctorates. "Tunisia is a country with a profound desire for education, Jazi said. "The only choice the government had was to create the possibility to provide education to all those who have the ability." So far, the state has borne the cost, but during 1997 there were exploratory talks about creating private educational institutions.

Among the ministries created after Ben Ali's takeover was the Ministry of Professional Training and Employment, headed in 1997 by Moncer Rouissi. He saw his task as that of creating a "market of qualifications," which led to the establishment of professional education centers parallel to the regular secondary-school system. The professional education network is linked by an agreement with employers' associations to coordinate the training in different fields and create what Rouissi called "an inventory of specialists."[10]

Feasibility studies have been conducted, and joint committees have been established, consisting of employers and representatives of different professions. In mid-1997, agreements existed in 11 different fields of economic activity and 35 centers of professional training were in operation. While previously trade schools were basically for those who failed academically, the picture has changed, Rouissi said: diplomas from professional trading centers are considered as equal to academic degrees. (The standard trade diploma is known in French as *"certificat d'aptitude professionelle* and is equivalent to two years of secondary education. A higher diploma is *"brevet de technicien,"* equivalent to the baccalaureate usually obtained at the end of secondary education.)

There is no age limit for students at the professional training centers, Rouissi said, and they are allowed to interrupt their studies and return later. "The system is intended to guarantee employment," he said, and the government "is trying to follow the labor market and keep a balance between the training and work opportunities."

Nothing illustrates better Tunisia's leap into the modern era than the transformation of the role of its women. From a male-dominated society at the start of its independence, Tunisia has fully integrated women into its economy, liberal professions, and the educational system. In 1997 there was no field of activity in which Tunisian women were absent. There were women magistrates, company executives, research scientists, specialists in genetics such as Habiba Chaabouni, and a pilot on regular Tunis Air Airbus flights, Selma Chetali. Polygamy was abolished in 1956, and, under a "Personal Status Code," Tunisian women have acquired rights which few other Arab countries have even contemplated.

In 1992, the parliament further consolidated the already impressive gains for women's rights by adopting a set of laws among the most progressive in the world. Thus, in the event of divorce, custody of the children no longer automatically goes to the husband. Violence against women within the family is punishable, and women can obtain passports without permission from their husbands or fathers. Divorced women can appeal to the state for help in case of alimony problems.

By contrast, in mid-1997, the women in "brotherly" Morocco were still considered as second-class citizens. In August 1997, a Reuters news agency dispatch said,

About 70 percent of them [Moroccan women] are illiterate. They cannot divorce, and they need their father's permission for marriage even at the age of 40. Up to 1993, they could not travel abroad without the approval of their guardian, who can be father, brother or husband. . . . The law also allows polygamy—with the only change to the original Sharia [Islamic law] being that a man now has to warn his wife of his plans to take another woman.[11]

Bourguiba, a man of considerable vision in the earlier years, launched a bold family planning program subsidized by the state and accessible to all. In the early 1960s, clinics dispensing contraceptives and offering advice on all forms of prophylactics were established in all Tunisian towns. In the 1990s nurses, paramedics, or midwives administered contraceptives, even in remote villages. Bolstered by a sustained health program, Tunisia soon reduced its galloping population growth of 3.2 percent to 1.9 percent. By 1993, "the birthrate has declined from 45 to 25.4 per thousand, [infant] mortality from 15 to 6.1 per thousand. The illiteracy rate has been brought down from 87.7 percent to 37 percent, though the figure is higher in poorer country areas."[12]

The involvement of women in Tunisia's political life has been generally limited, a fact often deplored by female activists and government officials. Among the reasons were lack of interest and of experience. Among Ben Ali's recent directives was one urging all his cabinet members to include women on their staffs.

There are, as usual, notable exceptions, such as Chadlia Boukhchina, deputy speaker of parliament, and Fathia Baccouche Bakhri, a lawyer and one of several parliament members. "We are still experimenting and the party [RCD] expects to evolve, eventually creating other groupings and different tendencies," she said.[13] Government officials, however, like to point out the considerable growth of female participation in elections. For example, while only 260,000 voted in the 1989 legislative elections, their number grew to more than a million in the 1994 vote. It was interesting that the winner in legislative by-elections in the province of Ben Arous in 1997 was Arbia Ben Ammar, a woman opposition candidate and human rights activist. During the 1995 municipal elections, RCD party "lists" included 644 women out of a total of 4,074 candidates. The proportion of women members in municipal councils grew from 14 percent in 1990 to 19 percent in 1995.[14]

By 1993 women held 25 percent of all jobs in Tunisia, 35 percent of jobs in industry, 22 percent in the services sector, and 40 percent of jobs in agriculture. A growing number of women have since formed small companies, including a major shipping company, a porcelain factory, an ice cream plant, and a fruit-exporting firm.

Not surprisingly, the arrival of this "new class" on the labor market of a small Arab country has caused comment—and frequently applause— throughout Africa, the Middle East, and parts of Europe. A typical reaction was one in the French-language monthly *Arabies*, describing Hayet Laouani, director and chairperson of the board of the maritime agency *Stumar* employing 172 workers:

Port of Rades. A giant Caterpillar. At the control, a petite dark-haired woman in an elegant but functional red ensemble. Surprising? Not really, when you know what kind of woman we are talking about. Hayet Laouani explains: "I have fallen in love with this job." True, only real love could have forced her to overcome the insurmountable or quasi-insurmountable obstacles in her path.

According to the magazine, Hayet began work at the age of 19 as a bilingual secretary in a small office she shared with three men, all of whom wanted her to become a telephone operator instead. She asked her supervisor for work in the docks. Her arrival there caused a near riot. Everyone was against her in that masculine milieu: policemen, employees, seamen. They did not like the fact that she bicycled to work. She almost quit but the following day, after a sleepless night, she returned. The torment lasted three weeks. "Then I made my decision: I will go to the bitter end, until they've accepted me." She struggled to learn "maritime English." She did not watch television, but she read. She carried her small son in a basket to work. "I didn't take any leave so no one could accuse me of anything."

The massive and increasing role of Tunisian women in the economy and in education was regarded by many diplomats and analysts as perhaps the most important single obstacle to Islamic fundamentalism. In an assessment of Tunisia's economic prospects in view of a possible Islamic threat from Algeria, a World Bank official listed the growing influence and importance of women as a barrier that no Islamic regime could ever cross.[15] It was mainly with women in mind that the government banned references to male superiority and the stoning of adulterous women from Arabic-language textbooks. Books by some key ideologues of modern fundamentalism were withdrawn from schools and public libraries.

One of the most vocal opponents of fundamentalism is Faiza Keffi, in 1997 president of the National Union of Tunisian Women, an organization pledged to further advance the role of women. Energetic and equally erudite in French and Arabic, she believes that there is only one way of coping with fundamentalism: defeat it. Her headquarters at 56 Bab Benat Boulevard is a hive of activity where women assistants draft more ambitious programs, plan international conferences, and answer questions ranging from child support problems to professional advice. "We are far ahead of the Arab world," Mrs. Keffi said.

In most Arab countries a woman depends on a man—the decider. All legislation is shaped from the masculine point of view. In Tunisia the man is still head of the family but the woman is a partner, participates in decisions on the education of children and, frequently, on family budget.[16]

The Union periodically conducts surveys among women and their male partners to monitor the evolution in attitudes and conditions of marriage as well as women's professional achievements and interests. The most recent survey published in a glossy, well designed book of 164 pages is entitled *L'Image de la Femme dans la Société Tunisienne* (*The Picture of Women in Tunisian Society*). Its statistics are highly revealing. For example, 51 percent of Tunisian women still contracted arranged marriages but only 47 percent in urban areas. Among those who freely chose their spouses, 16 percent met them at work and 58 through family acquaintances. Among urban women, 30 percent married for love, 43 percent because of the potential husband's social status, and 14 percent because of his financial situation.

Among modern Tunisian couples, 32 percent of conversation concerns their children, 30 percent their relationship, and only 16 percent general social and political problems. Such a pattern follows closely the tendency of most couples in industrial European countries.[17] Fifty-seven percent of Tunisian women believe that the husband should be the family's main bread winner while in rural areas the percentage rises to 64. In urban areas 39 percent of women believed that major decisions should be made by the husband because of the male superiority, while 36 percent claimed that they should because of the male's status as head of the family.

While 14 percent of the husbands interviewed in the survey would like to see their daughters reach high executive levels (*cadre*) in business, the percentage of mothers favoring such an ambitious career was 21. The dominant idea of a profession for women among both rural and urban married couples was teaching. The earlier resistance to career or even employment of women has been replaced by concern that women should have "a respectable profession."

No picture of Tunisia's nation-building would be complete without mentioning the role of Tunisian Jews, one of Judaism's oldest communities. As mentioned earlier, most Tunisian Jews left the country in the early stages of independence, driven either by economic difficulties and lack of prospects, or by fear of repercussions of events which affected relations between the Arab world and Israel. Thus the first significant exodus took place after the 1956 Suez Canal crisis, and the second after the battle of Bizerta. Then came the 1967 six-day war. Excited and frustrated crowds burned and looted Jewish shops. Although there were no victims, fear gripped the Jewish community and caused more departures. "This is not a violent nation and these riots are unusual," a senior member of the Jewish community said at the time. "But we see no prospects here for our children."[18] Subsequently, the remaining Jews were alarmed when the Palestine Liberation Organization moved from Beirut to Tunis.

More than a thousand Tunisian Jews remained nonetheless on the island of Djerba, home of one of the oldest synagogues, the famous Al Ghriba, initially built by Jews who came to Tunisia at the time of the destruction of the first temple in Jerusalem. Those Jewish silversmiths, artisans, and merchants in traditional dress added color to Djerba, which was becoming one of the major tourist attractions. Bourguiba was not interested in either attracting more Jews or in getting rid of the remaining ones. Those who stayed simply vegetated, a people without a future.

The Ben Ali regime took a different course. In October 1994, while visiting Washington, Habib Ben Yahia, then foreign affairs minister, launched an appeal to Tunisian Jews to "resume their ancient links with this open, tolerant country of theirs." He also called for a "reconciliation of the sons of Abraham," and said Tunisia would send a top-level trade mission to Israel to examine the possibility of joint ventures with the Jewish state.[19]

In 1996, Ben Ali gave the Jewish community $50,000 to renovate the Great Synagogue in Tunis. Another synagogue in Le Kef near the Algerian border had been restored previously and work was scheduled to begin on one in La Goulette along the Tunis seashore, once a traditional Jewish suburb. Also scheduled for restoration were a home for Jewish elderly and a cemetery in Tunis.

According to a report by B'nai B'rith in the United States, in Tunisia, "Jewish students enjoy a condition found rarely outside the United States: the right to take examinations on days that do not conflict with Jewish holidays." In December 1996, a Tunisian government spokesman described Jews as "an indigenous segment of society with full-fledged rights."[20]

While it is too early to say how many Tunisian Jews, now well established either in Israel or in France, would return, there were signs that the Djerba Jews no longer doubted in their future. "They no longer put their money under the mattress, they are investing in real estate and building homes," said Dr. Gabriel Kabla, a Djerba-born physician and head of the Association of Tunisian Jews.[21] Djerba, and particularly the Al Ghriba, attracted a steady stream of pilgrims from Israel. During 1996, some 5,000 Israelis visited Djerba.

The Tunisian Jewish community now settled in France maintains close links with Tunisia, where some still keep property and funds. Thousands of Tunisian Jews spend summer holidays in hotels along the Tunis coast. Tunisian officials regularly attend cultural events periodically organized in France to mark the "continuing relationship of the sons of Abraham."

NOTES

1. *Jeune Afrique*, 20 March 1996.

2. Mohammed Ghannouchi in *The Washington Report on Middle East Affairs*, November–December 1996.

3. Ibid.

4. *The Washington Report*, November–December 1996, p. 87.

5. Rachid Driss in conversation with the author.

6. *Jeune Afrique*, 20 March 1996.

7. Hatem Ben Othman in conversation with the author.

8. Mohamed Harmel in conversation with the author.

9. Dali Jazi in conversation with the author.

10. Moncer Rouissi in conversation with the author.

11. Reuters dispatch published August 30, 1997.

12. *Financial Times*, 14 June 1993.

13. Fathia Baccouche Bahkri in conversation with the author.

14. Tunisian government figures.

15. In conversation with the author.

16. Faiza Keffi in conversation with the author.

17. *L'Image de la Femme dans la Société Tunisienne*. The Tunisian Women's Association, Tunis, p. 30.

18. The member of the Jewish community in conversation with the author.

19. Habib Ben Yahia in an interview in *The Washington Times*, 7 October 1994.

20. Author's dispatch to *The Washington Times*, 14 December 1996.

21. Gabriel Kabla in conversation with the author.

CHAPTER 10

Preserving and Enriching

Old ramparts are being restored throughout Tunisia. Inhabitants of the *medinas*—those ancient warrens of narrow streets and traditional, squat houses—are encouraged and even helped not to abandon them. Outside the medinas which symbolize the past and attract tourists, ambitious and innovative architects are constructing a new, modern Tunisia with a strong accent on its heritage.

Apart from an effort to develop and streamline the country's economy in the face of globalization and increasing bonds with the other Mediterranean countries, Tunisia has launched a vast program characterized by measures to enhance the preservation of its ancient patrimony combined with intensified cultural activities. According to a Tunisian official who participates in organizing various international activities and archaeological trips, "a whole, new cultural dynamic is being developed."

During 1997, Tunis was designated by the United Nations Educational, Scientific, and Cultural Organization (UNESCO) to be the "cultural capital" of the southern shores of the Mediterranean. A series of seminars and conferences marked the year, together with literary, artistic, and theatrical performances.

Before the latest cultural activities were launched, Tunisia presented its program of urban and rural improvement at the Second United Nations Conference on Human Settlements in June 1996. The program aimed "to guarantee the basis for a harmonious development and to promote human rights in a sound and safe environment." It stressed that a whole package of government activities was directed "at the development of social housing, the consolidation of socio-collective facilities and the improvement of living conditions in urban areas and the construction of a balanced society, with priority being given to the human and social components in the development policy of the New Era."[1]

As expected from all official documents presented at international fora, this one stressed the role of Ben Ali and that Tunisia was a Mediterranean, African, Islamic country, as well as an heir to an impressive mix of cultures and civilizations. Nonetheless, what many Tunisians regard as *la langue de bois*—wooden language—hides a sustained and costly effort to pull the country up to the level of its northern neighbors in the Mediterranean, or perhaps even to surpass them.

The ultimate objective, of course, is not so much to impress the outside world as to create a healthy and safe environment for Tunisia's nine million people, the kind of environment that would reject any form of extreme political ideology or violence.

Thus, as the millennium is drawing to a close, Tunisia's social and cultural programs include efforts to preserve the heritage, protect the environment, and improve the well-being of its citizens. The usual official self-congratulatory statements apart, it can be objectively stated that, given its limited means and growing expectations of an increasingly educated young population, Tunisia was coping exceptionally well.

According to Ali Chaouch, minister of equipment and housing, "Tunisia is a vast construction site, driven by a desire to build a modern country in all possible dimensions. Everything is included: conservation of historic sites, construction of roads, motorways, dams, sports stadiums, hospitals and schools—anything that helps the country to develop in a balanced manner."[2]

In the ambitious plan adopted by the government, one of the main elements is what Tunisians call "social housing" or "human settlements." Every city has "a master plan of urban development, with strict rules about height, density and nature of housing depending on the area, avoiding anarchy and creating a satisfactory standard of living," Chaouch said.[3] According to the census of 1994, some 80 percent of Tunisians owned apartments or houses. The traditional trend to ownership is encouraged by the government through loans on relatively easy terms and the expansion of infrastructure such as roads, water supply, and electricity in new urban and rural housing projects. The capital, Tunis, is growing at a rate of 2 percent a year and reached, together with suburbs forming the metropolitan area, 1.8 million inhabitants. The city of Tunis alone had a population of 674,000 in 1997. But, Chaouch said, "as living conditions in the countryside improve, fewer people want to move to the cities."[4] Still, 61 percent of Tunisia's people are urban dwellers—a dramatic change since independence, and the government would like to stop or at least reduce the drift toward the cities.

In a report presented to the Habitat 2 conference in Istanbul, the Tunisian government estimated the country's urban population at 5.36 million and said that "Tunisian towns are growing at a rapid pace with an annual growth rate of 3.8 percent against a mere 0.4 percent in rural districts." The report stated that "the total number of urban housing units increased from 1,021,800 to 1,870.100 units between 1975 and 1994, which represent an increase of 45.3 percent against a 40.4 percent increase in the number of households over the same period."[5]

Parallel to the urban development program is a plan to improve country dwellings, particularly in what the government calls "shadow areas" or "zones of darkness" (see Chapter 8). The financing of the program includes assistance paid in five installments according to the progress of the construction.

"The dwelling should be self-built with the technical support of the administration."[6] In 1995, 84,000 rural dwellings were completed, or about 11 percent short of the initial target. The report stressed the importance of the role played by the National Solidarity Fund, commonly known as 26–26 (see Chapter 8). It emphasized that the rural improvement program be accompanied by a similar effort in favor of human resources. The target of the plan "is to promote citizens' awareness, develop their skills and promote their integration in the societal project of the new era the bases of which are self-help and rehabilitation through work."[7]

While it would be impossible to include all facets of Tunisia's wide-ranging social program, the expansion of the Social Security system and of the health program deserves special mention. Public health spending has been growing by 15 percent a year, allowing the poor to have access to free medical care. Currently, some 11,800 poor families receive completely free medical care, while 694,000 other families have access to public hospitals for a minimum annual health-care contribution.[8]

The social security system has been expanding at a similar rate, guaranteeing coverage and old-age pensions to growing numbers of workers. Thus, between 1987 and 1996, coverage was extended from 55 percent to about 70 percent of Tunisia's work force. At this writing, plans were under way to extend coverage to the self-employed in the agricultural and non-agricultural sectors.

While new "satellite" settlements, complete with shopping malls and fast-food cafes, are constructed around Tunis and apartment blocks are rising next to the ancient *ribat* in the heart of Sfax, the question of preserving the nation's heritage is also given considerable attention. It does not only concern the renown Roman and Punic ruins with their arches, amphitheaters, and other memorable monuments of the past millennia. Some Tunisians consider the preservation of their old cities dating back to the Middle Ages, the famous *medinas,* as equally important.

In Arabic, the term "medina" means simply the town. Before the colonial period, all Tunisian towns were "medinas," consisting of narrow streets, low houses often with inner courtyards, large doorways decorated with hand-painted tiles, windows protected by elaborate iron grills, and *mouch-arabiehs*—balconies surrounded by exquisitely carved wooden frames from which women could watch, unobserved, life in the street below. From the street milling with humanity and echoing with shouts of vendors and greetings, the facades of these houses do not, generally, look memorable. The beauty is mainly inside, and the wealth and status of the owner was demonstrated by the size of the courtyard, the fountain usually set in a tiled pool, the richness of decoration, and the colors and design of the ceramic tiles, often covering entire walls. There are also the *souks* or markets, some of them covered with wickerwork roofs to protect them from the heat of the blistering sun, and elaborate palaces of the rich, as well as mosques with their typical North African square-shaped minarets, solid government buildings, and *hammams* (public baths). The medinas survive to this day; however, now they are equipped with running water and electricity and, more and more frequently, with satellite dishes. Some of the finest architecture of the Arab world is in the medinas, and the configuration of those, frequently walled-in, cities has not changed for centuries.

The colonial period brought a new concept of living. New cities with broad, palm-lined avenues and tall buildings designed by European architects were constructed next to the medinas. These "European cities" soon became "dynamic poles of economic activity whose development has been directly proportional to the decline of the old centers. The medina has lost its former political status, and its role has been reduced to one of secondary importance—that of a residential district of the Arab-muslim population."[9]

As the concept—and very existence—of the medina remains very much part not only of Tunisia's past but of its present urban existence, the comments contained in Serge Santelli's work *Medinas, Traditional Architecture of Tunisia*, are worth citing again:

The new European quarter, with its up-to-date public and commercial amenities—railway station, bank, post office, town hall, etc.—has thus taken over the medina's traditional role and channelled off the principal activities within the urban agglomeration. The colonial city has thus become the standard urban and architectural reference for the Tunisian itelligentsia. Apartment buildings with decorated facades, monumental public buildings and residential villas have been imported wholesale; despite occasional arabesque treatment of the facades, they have been based entirely on European spatial models. The modern city, up-to-date and dynamic, thus stands in contrast to the medina, a symbol of the archaic past.[10]

It was inevitable that with the passing of the colonial era, the Tunisian "new class" moved out of its previous, somewhat ghetto-like and restricted existence, and into the wider and more open "European" part of the cities.

These new areas offered not only more comfort but also better facilities for administering a new nation and participating in its development and modernization. Consequently, the medinas have become the homes of the poor and underprivileged—as well as magnets for the growing number of tourists in quest of a glimpse of a different, more colorful world of the past. The fact that Tunisian medinas, unlike their Egyptian or Syrian counterparts, are generally clean and their inhabitants welcoming, facilitated their becoming a major tourist attraction and source of income for its merchants and traders, quick to pick up foreign languages.

Santelli complains in his work published in 1992, that, nonetheless, the image of the medina has been

aggravated by another image: that of a poor, insalubrious, damp and uncomfortable environment. Although some palaces and monuments have been restored, the vast majority of traditional houses and public buildings are now in an alarming state of disrepair, or even decay. The lack of upkeep, together with various repairs, modifications and transformations carried out by the inhabitants themselves, have irremediably disfigured both the outward aspect of the medinas and rural agglomerations, and the fragile, delicately ornamented interiors of the houses and other buildings.[11]

Whether or not prompted by such a harsh description or by other factors, the medinas are no longer forgotten in Tunisia's urban planning. According to Chaouch, the minister of equipment and housing, the main idea is to preserve the medinas as living and functioning parts of the urban centers with their specific architecture but with modern installations. In order to achieve this, conditions must be created to encourage people to remain in place, maintain their often crumbling dwelling, and improve them whenever possible but within the strict framework of the surrounding environment.[12]

Already back in 1967, or 11 years after independence, the Association for the Safeguarding of the Medina (ASM) was formed with the role of participating in all work aimed at restoring what can be restored and making sure that all new housing within the medinas conformed with the traditional aspect.

As one example of its activities, the ASM drafted an ambitious plan for the transformation and improvement of the El Hafsia quarter of the Tunis medina, completed in 1993 after 13 years of work. Details of this project were submitted in Tunisia's report to the 1996 Habitat 2 conference in Istanbul, which stressed that

the scope of this project consisted of integrating the old residential districts in the socio-economic network of the city, and assuring a better utilization of the central urban space by putting an end to the degradation of those quarters, reviving and transforming them into a salubrious environment.

The project, considered to be exceptionally successful, deserves more than a cursory mention. Originally, El Hafsia was the quarter of the Jewish community of Tunis. Following the establishment of the French protectorate in 1881, a number of well-to-do Jewish families gradually moved to the modern, western part of the city. The poor left behind had

insufficient means for the maintenance of their houses, which resulted in the degradation of the whole quarter; this induced the French authorities in the 1930s to declare them insalubrious residential areas, in danger of ruin and to propose their destruction.[13]

Subsequent efforts to salvage El Hafsia were limited and included a handful of dwellings as well as the construction of two schools and of a market. When plans were drafted in 1981 for a major transformation and improvement of the area, the World Bank agreed to finance about 40 percent of the estimated $13.3 million of the cost, which included the rehabilitation of 600 dwellings and the renovation of 500 additional dwellings and 150 small shops.[14]

The El Hafsia project, which preserved the style and architectural characteristics of the area, was awarded the Islamic Architecture Agha Khan Prize in 1983 and 1995.

A different form of improvement of the traditional urban areas concerned the so-called *ukalas*—dwellings sheltering four or more families not linked by kinship. The initial of the three phases of the $30 million project, which ended in 1997, included the rehabilitation of 15 such buildings and the destruction of structures considered to be overcrowded, lacking basic modern facilities and threatened with irreparable decay. At the time of the launching of the project, the ukalas housed some 15,000 people, most of whom had drifted to the capital in the 1960s. They were re-settled in housing estates built according to the traditional pattern—one-story self-contained small houses with walled courtyards. The ukalas worth preserving had thorough face-lifts, which included ornate facades with colored tiles and iron grills on the balconies.

Another example of how Tunisia preserves its archaeological heritage is the village of Sidi Bou Said, about ten miles from Tunis on a hill rising steeply above the sea. The "magic village" to Western poets and writers, the "seat of virtuous men" in old Arabic documents, Sidi Bou Said during the pre-colonial era was the summer residence of senior officials and rich merchants avoiding the heat of the Tunis medina. Its ancient, often multi-storied white-washed houses, gently sloping toward the sea, are decorated with tiles hand-painted in Nabeul. The massive ornate doorways and shutters on the windows are strikingly blue—known as "Sidi Bou Said blue." The village winds around the crest of the hill, and the view from it is probably incomparable, particularly toward the north over the blue waters of the bay of Tunis, with the greenery of Cap Bon opposite and the towering

Bou Cornine mountain. To those who know Sidi Bou Said, the view surpasses that of Naples.

During the colonial period and, subsequently, after independence, a number of modern villas were constructed but usually outside the small village with its narrow cobbled streets. They included the impressive residence of the U.S. ambassador, which overlooks the sea. Many of these new structures were built in traditional Tunisian style. The village maintains a strict rule about burying telephone cables, and houseowners are fined if they neglect to paint their houses, shutters, and window grills once a year. Since the early 1960s, Sidi Bou Said has attracted a mixed crowd of painters, writers, journalists, and others on the fringes of the literary or intellectual world. Rents were low (although they shot up in later years) and the village kept its incomparable charm. Jasmine-scented summer evenings echoed with songs from the Café des Nattes in the village center, and pipes shrilled when young boys rode to a circumcision ritual. It was a place where one could stare endlessly at the view.

Eventually the inevitable tourist buses started coming in. Some hole-in-the-wall grocers' stores were converted into shops selling handicrafts and the famous Sidi Bou Said bird cages, since imitated around the world. Nonetheless, the village continues in its old spirit, particularly since its appearance is largely due to one of its early foreign inhabitants, Baron Rodolphe d'Erlanger, who offered his palatial residence at the bottom of the hill to the government as a museum, provided the whiteness and the striking blue were maintained in the village.

The nature of this book, which concentrates mainly on the political and economic aspects of modern Tunisia, makes it impossible to describe completely the maintenance and restoration work carried on throughout the country which is dotted with ancient strongholds, ramparts, and *ribats* (fortifications), as well as with precious monuments of earlier civilizations. The world's richest collections of Roman mosaics are in Tunis and Sousse. Ramparts from a Byzantine citadel rise over Kelibia. Monastir, Bourguiba's birthplace, is surrounded by a magnificent ribat of the Aghlabite period dating back to the ninth century. Ruins of the miraculously preserved aqueduct which in Roman times brought water to Tunis still stretch for miles near the road to Zaghouane. The Roman amphitheater of El Djem is among the world's most impressive. All these require care and attention, and, despite some earlier neglect, the government is sparing neither funds nor effort.

Official policy is that the rich cultural heritage must be included in building a modern state. "We owe it to ourselves to include all components of our society, including previous civilizations," said Abdelbaki Hermassi, the culture minister.[15]

In the spirit of "hope for a new civilization of our Mediterranean,"[16] marvels of modern architecture are rising throughout Tunisia. While most utilitarian structures, such as hospitals, office buildings, schools, and banks keep an austere and functional appearance, there are notable exceptions. Tunisian architects appear to have been given free rein in their designs of hotels, blossoming across the country, particularly along its coastline and near the edges of the Sahara.

Resort hotels tend to be low, sometimes three-stories high, surrounded by greenery—and space. There is a tendency to mix highly futuristic designs with the Arabesque. This is also reflected in some housing projects in Tunis and Sfax. In individual buildings, architects like the idea of a central patio, very much like the Roman atrium, a concept typical of the Mediterranean area. For example, the Dar Midoun hotel on the island of Djerba is built around a patio surrounded by arcades on marble pillars. In the oasis of Tozeur, the walls of the Hotel Palmyre are decorated with an intricate local design in a color blending with the adjacent desert. The Hotel Sangho in Tataouine is built of red brick and gloriously blends with the surrounding stark scenery.

New residential areas in such cities as Tunis and Sousse reflect the Mediterranean and particularly the Arab tradition of a sober and functional exterior and intricate and heavily ornamented interior. This style is also reflected in structures such as banks and various, recently constructed official buildings, as well as as on university campuses.

The transformation of modern-age Tunisia, and particularly of its architecture, were perhaps best described by Roger K. Lewis, a man who, as a Peace Corps volunteer, designed his first projects in the 1960s in Nabeul, a town known for its hand-made pottery. He returned to Tunisia in 1997 and found a dramatically changed country.

"Although most of the projects—among them municipal auditoriums, schools, markets, public gardens and a beachfront hotel—I had designed and built 30 years ago were still standing, almost all have been transformed," he wrote in *The Washington Post*.

Many have been enlarged with additions. Some buildings, once standing on open sites at the edges of towns, have been literally swallowed up, absorbed by surrounding urban growth.

The few remaining substantially as designed have been cosmetically modified, their furnishings and colors altered, and housing functions completely different than first envisioned. . . . Architecture wasn't the only thing that has changed in Tunisia. . . . Villages have become towns, towns have become cities and cities have become sprawling metropolises. Fortunately, traditional urban cores—medinas and souks, or bazaars—are being preserved and continue to thrive. . . . Today the odors are gone. The country's infrastructure is better than [in] some European countries and comparable to many parts of North America.

And the former budding Peace Corps architect, now professor of architecture at the University of Maryland, concluded:

Last year the Peace Corps terminated its operations in Tunisia, symbolizing the end of an era. Tunisia seems virtually self-sufficient. The president of the Tunisian architectural association told me that Tunisia now has a thousand architects, most educated at the architectural school in Tunis. When I lived in Tunisia, there were virtually no Tunisian architects and no architectural school. For once, I was delighted not to be needed.[17]

The environment, often the victim in any race toward development, has not been forgotten in Tunisia. In 1991 Tunisia became the first Arab country to create a Ministry of the Environment in place of a previous government agency dealing with environmental problems. In 1996, a Center for Environmental Technologies was opened in Tunis to act as a Mediterranean-based training institution for other countries of the area.

When this work was being written, Tunisia had 50 sewage treatment plants in operation and planned to complete 40 more by the year 2000. According to officials, "not a drop of untreated sewage water reaches the Mediterranean in any Tunisian tourist area." Moreover, the treated water is also used to irrigate golf courses and urban parks as well as various crops not used for food production.

To propagate awareness of the environment and its importance to the planet, the government has created a cartoon desert fox called Labib, a sort of watchdog over proper environmental practices. Thus children have been heard warning parents "Labib won't like it," when they see garbage disposal not conforming to safe environmental practices. This Tunisian version of Smokey the Bear is a great television favorite during children's hour.

Tunisia's cultural program was accentuated by its role as the regional cultural capital in 1997. Exhibitions, lectures, and theatrical performances were staged, with the underlying themes of Mediterranean tradition and Tunisia's contribution to civilization throughout the Punic, Roman, and Arab period. The cultural program was "a search for the buried past," a theme the Tunisian media exploited to the hilt. At the outset of the busy year, the organizers included a filmed documentary entitled *From Carthage to Ben Ali*. The Tunisian president clearly decided to stay firmly in the forefront of such activities with a ringing speech on January 14, 1997. Ben Ali said,

Since the Change of November 7th, 1987, we have endeavored to free culture from the chains of monolithic thinking. . . . We have rehabilitated creators by giving them their due position and opening for them ways of creativity in freedom and serenity. . . . But the road ahead is still long, and the world around us is rapidly moving towards a model of globalization where only the best and the most capable will survive. . . . Thus we have linked the preservation of our heritage with bringing new blood into it so that it becomes a key factor of social progress and development, and a fundamental inspiration for cultural production, creation and innovation.[18]

So, once again, Tunisia's soldier-president seized the initiative in yet another field. Less charismatic than his predecessor, lacking Bourguiba's panache and erudition in the field of arts and letters, Ben Ali has managed to stay ahead in all facets of the country's wide-ranging process of building a nation and preserving its traditions. As he put it, "culture is synonymous with action and self-denial, and creativity is a painstaking effort. All who apply themselves to this task perform an act of allegiance to the nation, and deserve well of their country."[19]

NOTES

1. National Report for the Second United Nations Conference on Human Settlements, p. 7.
2. Interview with Ali Chaoudi in *Architecture Mediterraneenne-Tunisie*, February 1995, p. 14.
3. Ali Chaouch in conversation with the author.
4. Ibid.
5. National Report, p. 12.
6. Ibid., p. 23.
7. Ibid., p. 24.
8. Official government figures.
9. Serge Santelli, *Medinas, Traditional Architecture of Tunisia* (Tunis: Dar Ashraf Editions, 1992), p. 164.
10. Ibid.
11. Ibid.
12. Ali Chaouch in conversation with the author.
13. National Report, p. 70.
14. Ibid.
15. Abdelbaki Hermassi in conversation with the author.
16. Ben Ali in a statement, 1995.
17. *The Washington Post*, 14 June 1997.
18. Official text.
19. Text of Ben Ali's speech on culture.

CHAPTER 11

Into the New Millennium

As Tunisia marked the tenth anniversary of Ben Ali's government and its departure from the previous, post-independence, period of considerable uncertainty, the country appeared to be on the right track. A Third World nation with First World aspirations, Tunisia has chosen the challenge of association with Europe regardless of the cost and effort involved. The economic restructuring was bound to be painful, and various Western experts were unanimous that it could only be accomplished in an atmosphere of total political stability. Regardless of the obvious political limitations—by Western standards—of Tunisia's "presidential democracy," the regime introduced by Ben Ali seemed the best possible answer in the existing conditions.

The fact that a major political change, that of November 7, 1987, took place in complete calm, is outspoken enough. The system changed without any settling of old scores. A major political party—the only one that really mattered—was transformed into a new, modernized tool in the hands of the new head of state. Reforms giving the Tunisians the highest standard of living in their history were launched. Education continues to be one of the nation's priorities, as well as an economic advancement. Regardless of political affiliation or conviction, no legitimate opposition party has been capable of proposing a different or more logical course of action. The fact that the program is implemented by a well-established party *nomenklatura* inherited by the Constitutional Democratic Rally (RCD) from old Neo-Destour, may seem odd to some in the West but in Tunisia it has been accepted as part of the system since independence. Parties change, but their membership remains in place. That in itself is an interesting sociopolitical phenomenon.

Other problems remain, including Tunisia's "rough neighborhood" with its possible fallout; the existence of Islamic fundamentalism which, although thwarted in Tunisia, continues its struggle elsewhere; the economic difficulties of "coming up to the level"; and, finally, Tunisia's international credentials as a democratic nation.

Western chanceries have accepted the Tunisian political system as an essential intermediate step. They hope that as the country matures and develops economically, reaching the stage of a "young developed nation," the political spectrum will expand. For the time being the existing situation is regarded as the best possible environment for the country's economic progress. Its disruption would merely cause chaos and a major—if not disastrous—setback to Tunisia's recent achievements.

The question of Tunisia's continued political stability in the context of Ben Ali's possible succession is yet to be broached. Officially, a president (unless named for life, like Bourguiba), is to serve no longer than three five-year terms. Ben Ali's second mandate expires in 1999, before he has the chance to lead Tunisia into the next century and millennium, something that has been a strong theme during his presidency and of the political party he has created. There is no obvious successor on the country's horizon and the "closed circuit" political atmosphere simply precludes any discussion on the subject—unless it emanates from the Carthage palace itself. Ben Ali most certainly intends to run again—and win. The fact that no one even mentions the possibility of succession or replacement at the country's helm is a serious drawback for the "presidential democracy." In 1997 the authorized opposition parties were as mute on the subject as was Ben Ali's Constitutional Democratic Rally. In fact, the total silence on such a sensitive issue diminishes Tunisia's democratic credentials as it prepares to link its destiny with Europe. Mentioning the succession problem is virtually regarded as lese majesty. It is almost as impossible as press criticism of the head of state or, for that matter, of government decisions.

Ben Ali was only 51 when he took Tunisia's destiny into his hands. He is healthy, vigorous, and apparently works a 12-hour day. He is probably the best thing that has happened to Tunisia since independence. Bourguiba had a grand vision of what he wanted for the country, and some of the earlier accomplishments are entirely due to him. Later, however, the vision became blurred as old age destroyed the founder of modern Tunisia. Thus Ben Ali stepped in, a "man of his era," and put the wobbly house in order. The work is not finished, and a lot remains to be done. Perhaps it is true, as some say, that Ben Ali is the only man capable of making Tunisians work. He certainly is a no-nonsense, hands-on president who demands results and minces no words. In mid-1997 there was not the slightest indication that Ben Ali intended to relinquish power before Tunisia pulled itself "up to the level" of the countries it sought to emulate.

A constitutional amendment extending the president's term is most likely to be adopted to permit Ben Ali to accomplish the huge task he has set for himself and the country. There might be a referendum on the issue to make it perfectly legal, as is Ben Ali's custom. At this writing, there simply is no man in Tunisia likely to rise and announce his candidacy in a presidential election—unless designated by the ruling party and with Ben Ali's approval, as he indicated in his tenth anniversary speech.

In the event of an accident or unexpected sudden death, the president is to be succeeded by the head of the Chamber of Deputies until elections are called within two months. There is no precedent for such action. The president of the chamber, when this work was being completed, was Habib Boularès, an intellectual who managed to survive various vicissitudes during Bourguiba's rule and has emerged as a man Ben Ali trusts. He is more at ease at international conferences than at mass rallies. He is not known for harboring presidential ambitions—but neither is anyone else. Just before the tenth anniversary of the Change, Boularès was replaced by Fouad Mbazaa, a 60-year-old former minister of health.

In 1997, it was hard to imagine Tunisia continuing its economic progress without a man such as Ben Ali. There are a number of exceptionally capable men in the cabinet, but the dominant personality of the president has not created a climate propitious for anyone to demonstrate political ambitions other than those assigned from the top.

Tunisia's economic situation remains the dominant issue as the country prepares for the multiple challenges of the 21st century. Equally important is the long shadow of Islamic fundamentalism cast by neighboring Algeria. Since 1987, Tunisia has achieved political stability, something the entire political spectrum craved—with the exception of Islamic extremists whose designs have been blocked. "People here will give anything for stability, and now they have it," a Western diplomat who began and ended his career in Tunisia said. Discussing the Ben Ali regime, he described it as "a paternalistic government which acts as if it alone knew what's good for the country." Ben Ali himself, he said "is not necessarily loved but certainly respected." And, in summing up, he said Tunisia "is perhaps the only Arab country without oil capable of reaching prosperity—if it is allowed to stay on course."[1]

The country's economic growth of 4 percent per annum is encouraging and so are many factors such as "stability guided by a strong and omnipresent regime,"[2] proximity to Europe, a high degree of education, and a desire to develop along European lines. Among negative factors, at least in the late 1990s, were an inadequate and protected market, few natural resources, a manufacturing sector threatened by other countries with even cheaper labor, insufficient privatization of large enterprises, and those notorious and "difficult neighbors," Algeria and Libya.

Theoretically "united" in the Union of Greater Maghreb with Libya, Algeria, Morocco, and Mauritania, Tunisia is pursuing its development very independently. Over 90 percent of its trade is with Europe, most of it with France. Tunisian exports to France have been growing by 7 percent a year, including phosphates, ceramics, construction material, fish, dates, and olive oil. Economic relations with other Maghreb countries are minimal and stagnant, and with Morocco and Mauritania practically nonexistent. It is impossible to talk of any immediate improvement as all Maghreb countries have similar economies. Tunisia's economic interests lie in Europe and the government's policy is aimed in that direction. This tendency is bound to increase rather than diminish, with the concept of "Maghreb unity" remaining hardly more than a slogan.

Although many Tunisians remain highly critical of Gadhafi's Libya and chaotic Algeria, the former Tunisian minister and secretary-general of the Arab League, Chedli Klibi, believes that the concept of Maghreb "has not been disastrous." The Union "has not failed entirely, the causes of its stagnation lie elsewhere," he said.[3] "Bilateral relations are often jostled. Moreover, there are many reasons why Maghreb countries cannot decide to create a joint economy. Lack of confidence? Of course! The fact remains that trade exchanges have always been directed Northwards and it is difficult to change that."

Whether or not the Maghreb countries can ever become a successful target for Islamic extremists is a subject of considerable international debate. Libya remains an enigma as long as Moammer Gadhafi stays in power. In the mid-1990s all speculation about Libya's future was futile; its leader was as mercurial as ever but with considerably less international impact since the 1986 U.S. reprisal air raid that nearly cost him his life. Tunisia has been one of the main beneficiaries of Libya's low-key posture, particularly as, because of the 1992 United Nations flight embargo, it is the closest country from which Libyans can now travel abroad by air. In June 1997, Algeria held legislative elections that solved no basic or critical issues but merely gave a somewhat more "democratic" mantle to the army-backed regime. Morocco was ruled by an autocratic monarch who effectively suppressed an attempt at Islamic resurgence, again without definitive solutions. There was considerable concern in the West that the situation in Morocco was precarious. The country's size and ethnic diversity are such that, basically, little is known about the situation in the deep interior and the feelings of the population. Foreign chanceries preferred the relatively safe formula that Morocco would cope—as long as King Hassan remained on the throne.

In 1992, as Islamic-inspired terrorism gained strength in Algeria and Tunisia successfully stifled several fundamentalist plots, John L. Esposito wrote:

Islamic movements in the Maghreb, as in most of the Muslim world, have developed a new or modern Islamic form of organization. In contrast to traditional religious organizations, Sufi mystical brotherhoods [tariqah] and ulama associations active in the nationalist struggle, modern Islamic activist organizations have a lay rather than clerical leadership, are urban-based, and thrive primarily among students and educated professionals while also attracting members of traditional occupations [merchants, traders, craftsmen] . . . where governments permit, Islamic activists have moved from the periphery to the center and now participate in electoral politics and mainstream society. Most advocate working within the system rather than using violence to come to power.[4]

Five years later, such an assessment was no longer valid. In Tunisia and Algeria, political parties based on Islam were banned. In Algeria some political parties known to have Islamic links used different names to camouflage their true orientation. The extremists resorted to slaughter, thus alienating a large segment of the population. In Tunisia, economic advancement and effective security measures have reduced the Islamic movement to an insignificant political force. Fear of a situation similar to that of Algeria was widespread and many Tunisians spoke openly about "the plague of Algerianization." It was difficult to assess pro-Islamic sympathy on university campuses. Certainly the elite, with its Franco-Arabic education, showed no signs of paying heed to often hysterical slogans threatening Tunisia's modern achievements and promising, in effect, to turn the country into a medieval theocracy. While Algeria remained bereft of urgent social reforms, in Tunisia the mosque no longer had the monopoly of offering succor to the deprived. The state's social services and educational system have taken over. The progressive elimination of the "shadow zones" is an outspoken example.

Although some Western pundits still worried about a global, pan-Islamic surge that would threaten the West and its established order, according to all indications there was little room for any pan-Islamic or pan-Arab ideologies in modern-age Tunisia on the threshold of the 21st century. While no nation, regardless how strong or populous, remains safe from major currents sweeping either its neighbors or countries of similar faith, Tunisia looked sufficiently "vaccinated" against ideological or religious adventurism. Political vigilance and continued reforms were essential, though. Above all, the "coming up to the level" had to include urgent methods to reduce the ranks of unemployed, potentially a mass that could be maneuvered by expert salesmen of imported ideologies. And in this Tunisia was not alone. In 1997, the number of unemployed in the 15 European Union nations stood at 18 million. With their families, using the average figure of four per family, they represented 72 million dissatisfied people. Put together, they would form the Union's second largest nation, after Germany. In that sense, Tunisia's situation with its 350,000 jobless, some of whom had seasonal employment, was not that dramatic.

Inevitably, a lot depends on the situation in the rest of the Arab world, beyond the relatively limited confines of the Maghreb. For a number of years, the ups and downs of the Arab-Israeli conflict took their toll of Tunisia. The creation of Israel in 1948 caused the first wave of departures by Tunisia's native Jews. Others were to follow, particularly after the 1967 Arab-Israeli war. The hosting of the Palestine Liberation Organization after its exodus from Beirut in 1982 exposed Tunisia to Israeli reprisals. The Iraqi invasion of Kuwait and the resulting attack by a United States–led coalition on the Iraqi army created an embarrassing period in the normally warm relations between Tunis and Washington because of Tunisia's refusal to join or even approve the action. Given the notorious unpredictability of the Middle East, it is hard to predict a serene future.

As this book was being written, the wealthy oil states in the Gulf were facing a growing threat, mainly from highly organized Shias financed by Iran. Saudi Arabia was confronted by the difficult problem of succession, as well as by a considerable degree of economic stringency after years of lavish spending. The Saudi throne, balanced precariously on billions of barrels of oil, was by no means secure.

Fundamentalists were well entrenched in the Hezbollah movement in Lebanon as well as in the Hamas organization in the Palestinian self-rule territories. The policies of the arch-conservative government of Israeli Prime Minister Benjamin Netanyahu hardly encouraged a more durable relationship between Israel and its Arab neighbors. Although Jordan and Egypt have signed peace treaties with the Jewish state, by mid-1997 their relations were virtually frozen, limited to the presence of diplomatic missions and to the scheduled flights between Cairo and Tel Aviv.

Jordan's future in the late 1990s was also precarious, with Islamists, camouflaged or in the open, controlling most parliament seats in Amman. As in Morocco, the country's future seemed to depend on its monarch. Many observers were doubtful that the Hashemite dynasty would survive the demise of King Hussein.

Iraq and Libya remained international outcasts with the big powers unable to find any policy other than that of isolating the two major oil producers. Both, along with Syria, were considered by the U.S. State Department to be countries aiding and abetting international terrorism.

Syria, which exerted enormous influence—or control—over Lebanon, was in a state of readiness for yet another military confrontation with Israel. Its dialogue with the Jewish state was frozen in February 1996, and Netanyahu's election as Israel's prime minister in May of that year further removed the prospects of peace negotiations. Time and time again, Israel stressed its determination to hold on to the Golan Heights, a narrow strip of land it considered essential to its strategy and which Syria considered to be an inseparable part of its territory.

In the summer of 1997, Israel was unquestionably the volatile area's top military power, backed by billions of U.S. dollars and sophisticated equipment. On the other hand, the disintegration of the Soviet Union has deprived Syria of its major source of weapons supply.

This generally somber picture was further marred by the difficulties of the areas under the Palestinian Authority, rioting and Israeli reprisals in the parts of the West Bank it controlled, and the general disagreement on the future of Jerusalem. Amidst a steady flow of news of riots, arrests, and terrorist attacks plus a paralysis of the so-called peace process, it was difficult to show even moderate optimism about the future of the Middle East.

The purpose of stressing this depressing tableau is not so much to castigate the weakness of the Arab world as to show Tunisia's exceptional stability and steady economic progress compared to those of its Arab brethren. The author's conclusion is that the Ben Ali regime has created something unusually precious which should be preserved at all costs. Whether Tunisia is ready for what one Tunisian described as "the luxury of complete democracy" will one day be decided by Tunisians and their leadership alone. No amount of outside advice or patronizing comment serves any purpose. It is clear that the system is evolving and that it acknowledges its specific nature pending a wider "opening" along the lines of European democracies. The approaching association with the European Union will undoubtedly play a major role in such a transformation.

Here the floor should again be given to Robert H. Pelletreau, the man who served as U.S. ambassador to Tunisia during the four crucial years that saw the country's transformation, including the 1987 change of leadership. Visiting Tunisia in June 1997, he described Tunisia's situation as "speaking for itself."

"The rapid and efficient reforms launched by President Ben Ali allowed Tunisia to occupy a choice position on the international scene," Pelletreau told the Tunisian daily *Echourouk.*

What has happened in Tunisia is, without doubt, a model for developing countries. As far as the political situation is concerned, I am convinced of President Ben Ali's commitment to opening. He himself spoke of it to me a number of times. I have no doubt that Tunisia's political future will be a success, just as are its efforts to achieve economic development.[5]

The massive chant "Ben Ali—Tunis" of the crowds greeting the president in Sfax on that sunny April morning was more than a usual, well-organized welcome. It was a symbol of what is happening in Tunisia today. The name of the head of state has been linked with that of the country, obviously at his instigation. The two now seem inseparable, at least in the foreseeable future. And during the formative years ahead, Tunisia can only gain from this relationship.

NOTES

1. Richard Undeland, former public affairs officer at the U.S. embassy in Tunis, in conversation with the author.

2. *Le Moci (Moniteur du Commerce International)*, a French economic journal, 1 May 1997.

3. Chadli Klibi in an interview in *L'Economiste Maghrebin*, 4 June 1997.

4. John L. Esposito, *The Islamic Threat: Myth or Reality?* (New York: Oxford University Press, 1992), p. 152.

5. Robert H. Pelletreau in an interview in *Echourouk*, 17 June 1997.

APPENDIX A

Significant Dates

Significant dates in Tunisia's modern history:

1705–
1881   Ottoman Turks rule through the Husseinite dynasty of *beys*. The period was marked by the weakening of the power of Istanbul or "Sublime Porte," and the adoption of Tunisia's first constitution in 1861.

1881   French protectorate is imposed after an invasion by land and sea of colonial troops, mainly from neighboring Algeria. Beys remain as figurehead monarchs who "rule but do not govern." French control is made formal by the Treaty of Bardo.

1920   The liberal party known by its Arabic name Destour (Constitution) is created. The party spearheaded Tunisia's struggle for independence.

1924   Creation of the Tunisian General Confederation of Labor (*Confederation Générale Tunisienne du Travail*).

1934   The Destour Party is split and Neo-Destour Party is created at the congress of Ksar Helal.

1938   Major nationalist demonstrations in Tunis cause a French ban on Neo-Destour and the Labor Confederation.

1946   The General Union of Tunisian Workers (*Union Générale des Travailleurs Tunisiens—UGTT) is created.*

1948   Neo-Destour names Habib Bourguiba as its president.

1952   Members of the Neo-Destour Political Bureau, including Bourguiba, are arrested. UGTT calls a general strike. Unrest and armed resistance begins.

1954   French Premier Pierre Mendes-France recognizes the principle of internal autonomy for Tunisia in a speech at Carthage.

1955 Bourguiba returns from exile.

1956 Independence is proclaimed March 20. Bourguiba forms Tunisia's first independent government April 14.

1957 The bey is dethroned, and Bourguiba is designated president. Tunisia joins the United Nations.

1959 Tunisia adopts its first post-independence constitution on June 1. Bourguiba, unopposed, is elected president in November.

1961 Tunisian "death volunteers" fail to oust French troops from the naval base of Bizerta during a bloody five-day battle in July.

1963 The small Communist Party and the left-wing press are banned in January. The Destour Party becomes the "Socialist Destour Party" following a congress in Bizerta in October. Also in October, the last French troops leave Bizerta as the result of an earlier evacuation agreement.

1964 Tunisia nationalizes land held by French settlers. Economic reprisals by France follow.

1965 Bourguiba's tour of the Middle East and his call for recognition of Israel antagonize many Arab governments.

1967 Bourguiba suffers a major heart attack in March. In June, rioting sweeps Tunis after the Arab defeat in the war with Israel.

1968 Ahmed Ben Salah, minister of planning and economy who introduced socialist reforms, is removed and, subsequently sentenced to prison. He escaped five years later and fled to Algeria.

1970 Hedi Nouira becomes prime minister and launches a major program of economic liberalization.

1974 Bourguiba signs a short-lived "treaty of union" with Libya's Moammer Gadhafi.

1975 The constitution is amended to allow Bourguiba to become "president-for-life."

1976 Tension with Libya causes Libya to expel thousands of Tunisian workers.

1978 A strike called by the UGTT is drowned in blood and a state of emergency is proclaimed in January.

1979 The Arab League moves its headquarters from Cairo to Tunis following Egypt's peace treaty with Israel.

1980 Clashes arise in Gafsa with Libya-backed opponents.

1982 The Palestine Liberation Organization (PLO) moves its headquarters to Tunis.

1984 Riots caused by an increase in the price of bread erupt in Tunis.

1986 Student and labor unrest causes severe repression by the government.

1987 On November 7, Prime Minister Zine El Abidine Ben Ali removes Bourguiba from power, citing his incapability to govern. The act has been known since as the Change. Economic and political reforms follow.

Appendix B

Ben Ali's Takeover Address

The official English-language text of President Ben Ali's statement upon assuming power on November 7, 1987.

In the name of God, the Clement, the Merciful

We, Zine El Abidine Ben Ali, Prime Minister of the Republic of Tunisia, proclaim the following:

Fellow Citizens,

The great sacrifices made by the Leader Habib Bourguiba, first President of the Republic, together with other men of valor, for the liberation and development of Tunisia, are countless. And that is why we granted him our affection and regard and worked under his leadership for many years, confidently, faithfully, and in a spirit of self denial, at all levels, in the ranks of our popular and national army and in the government.

But the onset of his senility and the deterioration of his health and the medical report made on this called us to carry out our national duty and declare him totally incapable of undertaking the tasks of President of the Republic.

Thereby, acting under Article 57 of the Constitution, with the help of God, we take up the Presidency of the Republic and the high command of our armed forces.

In the exercise of our responsibilities, we are counting on all the children of our dear country to work together in an atmosphere of confidence, security and serenity, from which all hatred and rancor will be banished.

The independence of our country, our territorial integrity, the invulnerability of our fatherland and of people's progress are a matter of concern to all citizens. Love of one's country, devotion to its safety, commitment to its growth are the sacred duty of all Tunisians.

Fellow Citizens,

Our people have reached a degree of responsibility and maturity where every individual and group is in a position to constructively contribute to the running of their affairs, in conformity with the republican idea which gives institutions their full scope and guarantees the conditions for responsible democracy, fully respecting the sovereignty of the people as written into the Constitution. This Constitution needs urgent revision. The times in which we live can no longer admit of life presidency or automatic succession, from which the people are excluded. Our people deserve an advanced and institutionalized political life, truly based on the plurality of parties and mass organizations.

We shall soon be putting forward a bill that will concern the political parties and another concerning the press which will ensure a wider participation in the building up of Tunisia and of the strengthening of its independence in a context of discipline and order.

We shall see that the law is correctly enforced in a way that will proscribe any kind of inequity or injustice. We shall act to restore the prestige of the State and to put an end to chaos and laxity. There will be no more favoritism nor indifference where the squandering of the country's wealth is concerned.

We shall continue to keep up our good relations and positive cooperation with all other countries, particularly friendly and sister countries. We shall respect our international engagements.

We shall give Islamic, Arab, African and Mediterranean solidarity its due importance.

We shall strive to achieve the unity, based on our common interests, of the Greater Maghreb.

Fellow Citizens,

By the grace of God

We are entering a new era of effort and determination. Love of our country and the call of duty require this of us.

Long live Tunisia!

Long live the Republic!

APPENDIX C

Preamble to the National Pact

Official English-language text of the preamble to the National Pact, in which Tunisia's political parties agreed to cooperate with the government.

Taking inspiration from the authentic heritage of our civilization and from our glorious history,

Faithful to our brave martyrs and to all those who have fought, struggled and made sacrifices for the glory of Tunisia, for the dignity of the country's sons and daughters, and for its liberation from colonialism and dependence,

Out of regard for the men of rebirth and reform and for all those who have striven to build the republican system and established a State of laws and institutions, a guarantor of freedom and progress,

Putting into effect the principles stated in the Declaration of 7th of November 1987, which expresses the people's aspirations and guarantees them a dignified, modern way of life based on democracy, the multi party system, the sovereignty of the people and the primacy of law,

Aware of our historic responsibility at this turning point of our country's history,

We the representatives of the country's political parties and social and professional organizations, meeting on the first anniversary of the 7th of November, 1987 Change, do adopt this National Pact, pledging to take inspiration from it in our actions, and to comply with it in spirit and in letter, to disseminate its principles and objectives, and to consider it as a contract which binds us together and enables all Tunisians to participate in a single consensus, achieving a unity which is particularly important at the present decisive stage in our country's history, as we strive to usher in democracy and consolidate the legally constituted state, an undertaking that will require of us a minimum of understanding and concord.

We are concerned to establish traditions of fair competition. Firm in the conviction of our legitimate right to hold different opinions, signifying neither sedition nor rifts, we proclaim that our supreme goal is to fortify the foundation of the State—the State of all Tunisians—as a tool for achieving the ambitions of our people and for mobilizing all our energies and all our human and natural resources for the enhancement of Tunisia's place in the world and the realization of our desire to contribute to civilization, improve our security, and enable the Maghreb and the Arab world to recover its historic initiative and restore the influence of Islamic civilization.

Aware of the delicate nature of the transition stage we are now going through and of the many difficulties our country faces at this particular moment in its history, we consider it one of our most pressing duties to declare that a set of values concerning identity of the Tunisian people, the foundation of the political system, the principles and goals of development, and Tunisia's international relations, must be an object of consensus on the part of all Tunisians.

APPENDIX D

Questions and Answers

President Ben Ali's answers dated October 7, 1997 to written questions submitted by the author. (Author's translation from the French)

1. What prompted you to choose a military career?

Since my early youth, when I was in secondary school, I always dreamed of serving my country, my nation. My first opportunity to do so was to join the ranks of the nationalist movement. As Tunisia had just became independent, I thought the army offered me a chance to serve with honor and devotion.

2. Did you find diplomacy, as military attaché and then as ambassador, satisfying?

They say that diplomacy is the art of providing the best possible defense for one's country; it is also the art of representation, of negotiation, of compromise. Indeed, I learned all that during my diplomatic experience. Diplomacy particularly enriched my perception of different things, of means to best serve Tunisia's interests in a wider context which took into account the experience of others. A diplomatic experience also helps promote human relations and contacts with other cultures and political concepts, and contributes to the strengthening of peace, friendship, and cooperation among nations.

3. When did you decide to pursue a political career?

As far as I am concerned, there was never any question of turning politics into a career. More aptly, it was a concrete translation of the patriotism and of the taste for public service which I felt deeply. These feelings prompted me to join the ranks of the national movement when I was still in school, and later were responsible for my choice of military studies. A sense of political responsibility came later and was, from the very beginning, an answer to the call of duty.

4. What do you consider to be your most important accomplishment as minister of the interior?

No answer provided.

5. And as president?

It was a great satisfaction, which I am happy to stress, to have restored the confidence of the Tunisian in himself and in his ability to overcome obstacles. In fact, this restored confidence is at the root of the progress and changes accomplished by my country during recent years. By recovering hope in the future and self-assurance, the Tunisian has freed himself from doubt, found new taste for work, restored the confidence of his foreign partners and put to full use ancestral qualities, will power and knowledge essential to maturity and accomplishment.

6. You and your party are leading Tunisia into the 21st century. Does that mean you will seek another mandate as president?

No answer provided.

7. What obstacles do you see in the path of Tunisia's economic improvement ("mise à niveau")?

The major challenge is the unequivocal need to reconcile the continuation of economic reforms with the essential control over their social fallout. It is essential to make sure that these reforms do not cause painful consequences in the social domain and particularly in employment. This calls for a set of varied and complex reforms, structures and measures which we are in the process of launching, and various developments in the field of professional training, education, research, investment, propagation of small businesses, crafts, etc.

Other obstacles include the sensitivity of enterprises in the face of competition with all its implications, as well as an improvement of the administrative services and their regulations, easing of procedures, encouragement of private initiative and disengagement of the state in the non-strategic fields.

8. What do you regard as a potential external threat to Tunisia's security?

No answer provided.

9. On the political scene, is the RCD to remain as the country's framework party ("parti d'encadrement") in the future or do you see an evolution that would give more voice to the legal opposition?

The profound faith in the principles of democracy and political pluralism which we announced from the very beginning of the Change of 7 November 1987, has been translated, among other measures, into many legislative and constitutional amendments which have rapidly borne fruit. Thus pluralism was put into concrete form first in political life with seven legal parties, then with their participation in municipal and legislative elections and their entry into the Chamber of Deputies in

1994, for the first time in the history of modern Tunisia. We have also committed ourselves to encouraging the development of political life as well as promoting the participation of different groups in the running of public affairs, including the reinforcement of political parties through state financing. It is with that in mind that we announced, 28 December 1996, a set of initiatives in order to institutionalize political parties within the framework of the Constitution, as well as the reform of the Electoral Law to expand membership of the Chamber of Deputies and of other elected bodies. From there on, it is up to the political parties to work in order to expand their audience.

As far as the RCD is concerned, it is a majority party and, without doubt, will remain as such for a long time, particularly as it enjoys very large mass support and has frequently demonstrated the ability to evolve and develop its message and its audience.

10. With the elements at your disposal, how close is Tunisia to achieving the stage of a "young developed nation?"

During the past ten years, thanks to the adoption of innumerable reforms, Tunisia was able to free itself of the status of an under-developed country and reach one already quite enviable status [*sic*], that of an emerging economy. Unquestionably ambitious, the Tunisian nation is also realistic because it knows its capability and its possibilities and has confidence in itself. Thus it was decided to expand the objectives in order to join the developed nations. No, it is not a question of ambition but an objective which all Tunisians want to achieve.

In fact, we hope and are determined to reach this objective during the first decade of the coming century.

The following text was added in response to a faxed query by the author asking the president to describe his "personal feelings before and during the events of November 1987, in the face of domestic Islamic opposition and the influence of the neighboring countries":

From the beginning of my appointment as Prime Minister, I was able to realize the extent of the catastrophe which threatened the country. The situation was due to the bankruptcy of the policies pursued at that time, the paralysis of the state machinery, the resignation of the private sector, and the disappointment of the population.

Thus the first task of the Change of 7 November 1987 was to re-establish the confidence of the State in itself and between the State and the population, in order to extricate the country from stagnation and threats of all kinds, particularly the fundamentalist threat, and to launch the necessary reforms. The reforms were intended to endow the country with stable democratic institutions based on a democratic tradition and the most complete respect of human rights. It was also necessary to carry out a radical reform of the mental outlook, including a complete revamping of the educational system, of professional training, and scientific research. The general direction was that of modernization and adaptation to the new demands of the process of development and scientific progress in the world.

.

Bibliography

BOOKS

Ajami, Fouad. *The Arab Predicament*. Cambridge: Cambridge University Press, 1981.

Amami, Abdallah. *Le Mouvement Ennahda*. Tunis: Maison Tunisienne d'Edition, 1991.

Ayubi, Nazih. *Political Islam: Religion and Politics in the Arab World*. London: Routledge, 1991.

Balta, Paul. *Islam, Civilisations et Sociétés*. Paris: Editions Rocher, 1991.

Binder, Leonard. *Islamic Liberalism: A Critique of Development Ideologies*. Chicago: University of Chicago Press, 1988.

Burgat, François. *L'Islamisme au Maghreb*. Paris: Karthala, 1988.

Camau, Michel. *Pouvoirs et Institutions au Maghreb*. Tunis: Ceres Editions, 1978.

Chaabane, Sadok. *Ben Ali et la Voie Pluraliste en Tunisie*. Tunis: Ceres Editions, 1996.

Cooley, John K. *Baal, Christ and Mohammed: Religion and Revolution in North Africa*. New York: Holt, Rinehart and Winston, 1965.

———. *East Wind Over Africa: Red China's African Offensive*. New York: Walker and Company, 1965.

Dunn, Michael C. *Renaissance or Radicalism? Political Islam: The Case of Tunisia's al-Nahda*. Washington, D.C.: International Estimate, 1992.

Esposito, John L. *The Islamic Threat: Myth or Reality?* New York: Oxford University Press, 1992.

Gilsenan, Michael. *Recognizing Islam: Religion and Society in the Modern Arab World*. New York: Pantheon, 1983.

Hermassi, Abdelbaki, *The Islamist Dilemma*. London: Ithaca Press, 1992.

Hunter, Shireen T. *The Politics of Islamic Revivalism*. Bloomington: Indiana University Press, 1988.

Huntington, Samuel. *Political Order in Changing Society*. New Haven, Connecticut: Yale University Press, 1968.

Ibn Khaldoun. *Prolegomena*. Paris, 1934.

Lawrence, Bruce. *Defenders of God: The Fundamentalist Revolt Against Modern Age*. New York: Harper and Row, 1989.

Mayer, Ann E. *Islam and Human Rights: Tradition and Politics*. Boulder, Colorado: Westview Press, 1991.

Moore, Clement. *Tunisia Since Independence*. Berkeley: University of California Press, 1965.

Pipes, Daniel. *In the Path of God: Islam and Political Power*. New York: Basic Books, 1983.

Salem, Norma. *Habib Bourguiba, Islam and the Creation of Tunisia*. London: Croom Helm, 1984.

Santelli, Serge. *Medinas, Traditional Architecture of Tunisia*. Tunis: Dar Ashraf Editions, 1992.

Sivan, Emmanuel. *Radical Islam: Medieval Theology and Modern Politics*. New Haven, Connecticut: Yale University Press, 1985.

Teicher, Howard, and Gayle Radley. *Twin Pillars to Desert Storm: America's Flawed Vision in the Middle East from Nixon to Bush*. New York: William Morrow and Company, 1993.

Wright, Robin. *Sacred Rage: The Wrath of Militant Islam*. New York: Simon and Schuster, 1989.

Young, Desmond. *Rommel, The Desert Fox*. New York: Harper, 1950.

Zartman, William I. *Man, State and Society in Contemporary Maghreb*. New York: Praeger, 1973.

NEWSPAPERS AND PERIODICALS

Afrique Magazine (Paris)
Arabies (Paris)
Architecture Mediterraneene, Tunisie (Tunis)
Christian Science Monitor (Boston)
Echourouk (Tunis)
Economist (London)
Economiste Maghrebin, L' (Tunis)
Financial Times (London)
Foreign Affairs (New York)
Global Networks (London)
Ithaca (Paris)
Jeune Afrique (Paris)
Monde, Le (Paris)
Monde Diplomatique, Le (Paris)
MOCI (Moniteur du Commerce International) (Paris)
Newsweek (New York)
Nouvel Afrique Asie, Le (Paris)
Observer (London)
Presse, La (Tunis)
Reuters (London)

Revue de l'Entreprise, La (Tunis)
Solidarite Maghrebine (Tunis)
Wall Street Journal (New York)
Washington Post (Washington, D.C.)
Washington Report on Middle East Affairs (Washington, D.C.)
Washington Star (Washington, D.C.)
Washington Times (Washington, D.C.)

OFFICIAL PUBLICATIONS

Les Droits de l'Homme en Tunisie: Options et Réalisations (Tunis), government
    publication.
Human Rights in Tunisia: Choices and Achievements (Tunis), government publi-
    cation.
L'Image de la Femme Dans la Société Tunisienne (Tunis), government publication.
National Report for the Second United Nations Conference on Human Settlements
    (Tunis), government publication.
Reflections on Human Rights in Tunisia (Tunis), government publication.
Reforme de la Formation Professionnelle en Tunisie (Tunis), government publica-
    tion.
Tunisia: A Country That Works (Tunis), government publication.
Zine El Abidine Ben Ali: The Leader of National Renewal (Tunis), government
    publication.

Index

Carthage: in antiquity, 11, 12; Carthaginians, 11, 12; in modern times, 13, 15, 21, 32, 88, 104, 129; as presidential palace, 1, 4, 8, 36, 37, 53–56, 58, 68, 77, 80, 96, 102, 132
Catholic, 15, 17, 32
Chaabane, Sadok, 3, 71, 73–75
Chaabouni, Habiba, 114
Chad, 57
Chadli, Amor, 58
Chaker, Abdelmajid, 60
Chalons-en-Champagne (Chalons-sur-Marne), 70
Chamber of Deputies, 6, 72–75, 77, 133
"Change, the," 8, 24, 45, 53, 57, 61, 64, 70, 72, 76, 129; and Islamists, 49; and Maghreb, 86; measures of, 3, 5–6, 94; and the press, 80–81
Chaouch, Ali, 122, 125
Charfi, Mohamed, 49
Chetali, Selma, 114
China, 85, 92
Chou En-lai, 33, 85
Chourou, Sadok, 47
Christianity (Christians), 13–15, 48
Christian Science Monitor, 13
Citibank, 110
Columbia University, 80
Communist Party of Tunisia, 32, 62
Constitutional Council, 64
Constitutional Democratic Rally (Rassemblement Constitutionel Démocratique [RCD]), 5, 16, 20, 45, 46, 50, 60, 68, 71–73, 75, 101, 115, 131, 132
Cooley, John, 13
Council of the Republic, 33
Crimean War, 15
Cyprus, 26, 104
Czechoslovakia, 85

Damascus, 41
De Gaulle, Charles, 27–28, 30, 85
Desert Storm, Desert Shield, 46, 88 89
Destour Party, 36, 40, 54, 55, 60, 62, 70, 72; breakup of, 19; changes of, 16, 33; formation, 17; growth, 18; replaced, 20. See also Neo-Destour

Dido, 11
Djerba, 18, 24, 27, 34, 103, 117, 118, 128
Dougga, 12, 14
Dougui, Noureddine, 14
Driss, Rachid, 110
Dunn, Michael Collins, 9, 10, 50, 74

Eastern Europe. See Europe
Echourouk, 57, 137
Economist, The, 50, 59
Egypt, 12, 25–26, 28, 30, 32, 33, 68, 87, 104, 136; and Arab League, 87, 88
Eisenhower, Dwight D., 26
El Djellez cemetary, 17
El Djem, 14, 127
El Hafsia, 125–125
English language, 9, 79, 99, 107, 108, 109, 111, 113, 116
Ennahda, 45. See also Al-Nahda
Erbakan, Necmettin, 46
Erlanger, Baron Rodolphe d', 127
Eshmun, 11
Esposito, John L., 49, 134
Ettajdid Party, 73, 75, 113
Europe, 7, 9, 12, 14, 15, 20, 26, 49, 81, 84, 95, 99, 101, 108, 110, 115; as model, 109, 133; partnership with, 72, 131; in tourism, 104
European Union (EU), 86, 95, 98, 100; Tunisia's association with, 76, 85, 86, 95, 98, 100, 137; unemployment in, 135
Evian-les-Bains, 29

FIS. See Islamic Salvation Front
Fort Bliss, 70
Fort Holabird, 70
France, 13, 19, 70, 83, 101, 102, 112, 113; and Algeria, 7, 15, 19, 23, 26–28; and Ben Ali, 58, 59, 84; in Bizerta crisis, 29–30; invasion of Tunisia by, 16; protectorate in Tunisia, 13, 16–17, 20–21, 108, 126; relations with Tunisia, 26, 27–30, 32, 84; Sakiet Sidi Youssef attack, 27, 90; in Suez crisis, 26; and trade, 134; and Tunisian Jews, 118; and

ISBN 0-275-96136-2

90000>

EAN

9 780275 961367

HARDCOVER BAR CODE